A Passionate Love

BOOK ONE
OF THE *MASQUED LOVE* SERIES

KARIEMA TALIEP DAVIDS

First Printing: 2022

ISBN
978-1-7764030-7-3 (Print)
978-1-7764030-8-0 (Ebook)

Printed and Bound in South Africa by PRINT ON DEMAND

The author may be contacted at: dimebuild@mweb.co.za

DEDICATION

I dedicate this novel to my dearest husband Faiek Davids, who has been incredible in your patience and support. For all the hours you have sacrificed to me, and encouraged me in every way and believing in me and everything I dream of doing. To a special friend Dr. Ilyaas Parker, for using your institution for writing, my deep and heartfelt gratitude. And last but not least, my dear friend, Librarian Girl. There aren't enough words to thank you for all the hours you have invested in discussing and listening to me.

CHAPTER 1

It was a bitterly cold night in Campden, the Northern side of Hamstead. Rain was coming soon and it was bound to snow eventually. It's certainly not a good time to go out, but for Catherine Darcy Evans, tonight is important. Wearing a tight-fitting, winter white, knitted dress, a cape, her husband bought her, and three-inch heels. The hooded cape she threw over her shoulders to keep warm. She headed to the coffee shop. Fluffy flakes started to fall. Catherine parked her car close to the entrance and walked into the coffee shop. It was a weeknight so it wasn't very full. She nodded at the waitress who smiled at her. She went to sit right at the back corner table, overlooking the whole area of the restaurant. This was her favorite spot and it was very cozy. Exactly one year ago she was sitting with her husband Harold Evans. Tonight is her second wedding anniversary. Sadly, her husband was knocked down and tragically passed away, eleven months ago. The waitress came over.

"Hi, how are you, my dear?" Tessa asked with a friendly expression. "Rather cold and snowy tonight. Are you waiting on someone?" she asked.

"Hi Tessa, yes, I saw on the news, hey. No, it will only be me tonight. Could I order a latte and a slice of carrot cake, please? That would be all. Thank you, sweetheart." she whispered.

She can't believe she sitting all alone. She scrolled through her mobile phone, looking at videos and pictures of the good times they shared. Shedding a tear, smiling in between, and very sad. Tessa brought her coffee and cake.

"Enjoy, honey, call me if you need anything else." Tessa smiled.

"Thank you, darling." concealing and choking back her tears. The song 'Happy Anniversary' by Ray Goodman and Brown, played in her head. Harold played the song for her last year. She was sitting there for hours, reminiscing. Friends came in with their business associates. They discussed work matters, laughed, and had fun. On the opposite side, five guys were doing some networking. Each one of them had their laptop in front of them. Some of them were loud. She sighed, deeply.

"This is life. Short, lived happiness. It was the best time of my life. Happy heavenly anniversary, my love." she toasted.

After a while, four of the guys left. She noticed one of them still sitting on his own. He was a charming good-looking guy. She senses a stare and a magnetic force from this French stranger, glaring at her. She only noticed him now that the others left, and she realized, he was watching her all night. She called Tessa over.

"Could you please bring me the bill, honey?" she asked.

"Sure, will do," Tessa answered.

"Now for a hot bath and under the covers," Tessa said.

"I will do that." Catherine agreed.

She gave her a ten pounds tip.

"Oh my, thank you, thank you, my dear! May God bless you with all your heart's desires," she said happily.

Catherine smiled at her, took her bag, and walked to the car, not far from the entrance. To her dismay, her back wheel had a puncture. She had no choice, but to change the wheel. By that time, the French man, also left the coffee shop, on his way to his car, which was parked two cars behind Catherine's car. As she was struggling, he rushed over to her to offer his assistance.

"Oh, my goodness, thank you, Sir. You are God-sent. Hi, I'm Catherine, so very pleased to meet you." she, greeted and shook his hand, happily.

"Hi Catherine, I'm Jacques Dupont, the pleasure is all mine. Let's fix this baby for you," he said smiling.

She smiled straight back at him, a big open smile. She was a petite, brunette with a strong English accent. She gave him that look, that almost every girl who is interested, gave a man. His heart felt hollow. There was something special about this girl. She was like a species from another planet.

"I can't help by notice you sitting all alone all night. Is everything okay?" Jacques asked.

"Oh yes, I am fine, thank you for the concern. That's a long story. I don't feel like talking about it. We going to have heavy snowfall, apparently eight inches and it's late, I need to get home." she explained. "Here is my card, I have a boutique on Oxford Street, called H.E Fashion Boutique. Please pop around when you're in the area. Thank you so much, once again for your help." she said.

"You're welcome, for sure, you be safe now. See you soon." Jacques said with a big smile on his face.

"Wow, what a charming, sensuous man." Catherine, thinking out loud. She lives alone in a beautiful apartment in the City of London. On her way home, she could not stop thinking about this gorgeous-looking man. She jumped into the shower. Curled up in bed. She slept like a baby. The next morning, she woke up beaming.

For the first time in almost a year, she feels good and has a zest for life again. She had her coffee and could not wait to get to work. She dressed up very elegantly and stylishly today. It was a pleasant winter day. The snow removal trucks were already busy clearing the ice and the snow from the roads and sidewalks. She left early to open the boutique as she had some administration work to do. It's rather hard to concentrate, though, as all she could think of was Jacques. She feels like she's on another planet.

"What if I never see him again. I didn't take any contact details from him." she's thinking.

"Oh my gosh, what is wrong with me? I don't even know this man. What if he is married? What if he is a psychopath? I feel I have butterflies in my stomach just thinking about him." she told herself.

All right, it's back to reality. The staff arrived. She is very close to her staff since she lost her husband. For Catherine, treating her staff like family means demonstrating the core values of her business and empowering and trusting them. She gives them the freedom to be innovative and creative, and this is the key to leadership. They were Vicky, Amelia, Emily, Gary, and Albert.

"Hi guys, everyone greeted."

"Oh my, you look pretty awesome today. What's happening? Have you struck it lucky, Catherine?" Vicky asked.

"No way, she sneaked a shy look at Vicky and Emily. How are you ladies doing?" she asked.

"Great!" some of them replied.

She turned her gaze away from them and let it sweep over the crowd stepping into the shop. It was Friday, so it was rather very busy. She stepped out of the boutique for a moment, just to gasp some air. It's been a long morning for her. By early afternoon, the shop is now bustling with clients, regular clients, and new clients. They always looking for a new outfit for weekend parties and functions. As she turned around, there he was.

"Hey, excuse me, I am looking for the girl with the long hair," Jacques asked Emily with the most beautiful Parisienne accent.

"Good day to you Sir. There she is." Emily nodded at Catherine, rolling her eyes.

Catherine was now smiling from ear to ear. Heartbeat racing.

"Hey, what a nice surprise. How are you." she greeted.

"Hi Catherine, I'm well, thank you. I have an hour break, so I thought I'll ask you out for a coffee or lunch if you can manage?" Jacques asked nervously.

"I see your store is hectically busy. Very beautiful boutique you have here," he said.

"Thank you. No, no, we can go. I have enough staff on duty. Let's go." she replied.

Catherine took her bag and mentioned to the girls, that she'd be back in an hour. They all showed their thumbs up! The two of them left for a French restaurant in the city.

"So, what is it you doing?" she asked.

"I'm in the Dental industry. I have a practice at The Dental Centre. I am originally from Paris. My father is French and my mother is Italian. I was married for a few months and divorced for five years. What about you, are you seeing anyone?" Jacques asked reluctantly.

"No, I'm a free spirit kind of a woman. I was married for just over a year. My husband tragically died in a car accident. We were together for three years. He was a Mariner. I never really got over his loss. It's very difficult to move on." she said.

"I think we'll have coffee and I would like to invite you for dinner. You can say when you're free. I am an excellent cook. There isn't much time in an hour. I would like to get to know you better." Jacques said.

"That would be great, let's make it Saturday evening," she said loftily. She could feel his gaze on her. They connected instantly. He was very smart and funny. She loved this in a man. Someone who can make her laugh.

"You are quite an enchanting person and you look so beautiful," Jacques said.

They drove back to the boutique and he dropped her off. Their eyes locked in each other's gaze. There was a special connection here. "You're an incredible woman, Catherine. See you on our first date," he said excitedly. Take my card. I will call you." he told her.

"Could this be love? I am so attracted to this guy's personality. I can't wait to see him again." she told herself.

"Wow, wow, wow! That explains why you glowing and shining today, Catherine." all the girls cheered her.

"He is quite a hunk." the girls said.

Catherine's eyes were a little too bright, Vicky thought, but it's good. She needs this.

"Yes, we have a dinner date on Saturday night. He is cooking, I will bring the desserts. I'm so excited." she said.

"Lovely, hope you all of the best, be careful out there, though." the girls warned.

She still finds it hard to accept she was lucky she had a flat tire.

"Could it be fate or is it the prayer Tessa, the waitress gave her?" she thought to herself. Catherine and Jacques spoke for hours on the phone on Friday night.

Jacques: Hey, how are you, my dear?

Catherine: I'm good and you? You not canceling our dinner date, are you?

Jacques: No, of course not.

Catherine: Are you picking me up or shall I drive to your place? What dessert do you like? I will bring something sweet.

Jacques: I can pick you up, but if you prefer to drive over to my place, as long as you are here.

Catherine: All right, so I'll be seeing you around 7 pm sharp. I'll drive over to you.

Jacques: Great, I'll be delighted to have you here, see you soon.

This is the first time in ages Catherine is going out on a date. Suddenly she is super excited and apprehensive at the same time. Emotions are running high. In her lounge, she has pictures of her and her husband. Catherine knelt on the floor, looking at the frames.

"My dear Harold, you will always take a big place in my heart. A big part of me died, when you died. I am lost without your love. You are always on my mind and forever in my heart. I will always love you and treasure the life we spent together. I feel lonely and empty. I have to move on." Staring at his pictures for a while, she felt better. She's struggling to fall asleep. The next morning, Catherine is excited. She called in to tell the girls she won't be coming in. She decided to make a Chocolate Souffle. That is always a winner for a romantic dinner date.

Late afternoon, the dessert is ready. Catherine preparing for her date. Dressed up in a black, velvet dress, suspender pantyhose with high heels. She wore her favorite perfume, La Vie Est Belle. She's ready to go.

It's Saturday night after 6 pm. The roads were rather busy. Catherine arrived at Jacques's place. She could smell the aroma from outside. She rang the bell.

"Hey, hey. I'm a little early, but don't mind me if you are not ready with food. Oh my, it smells divine. The aroma just gets to me as I walked in from the outside."

"Hi, Catherine, and dinner is just done. So good to see you. Thank you for the dessert, it looks great."

A few minutes later he was drawing her into the dining room. The gas-fire logs were lit. The table is set with lit candles, delicate dinnerware, and cutlery. Soft music playing.

"Shall we have a drink before dinner?" he asked.

"On the contrary, I'm starving. Let's eat," she said.

"You cooked up a storm here, hey. Food for the whole neighborhood."

Catherine was amazed. They had the easy starters, the main course. French mustard chicken, some herby salad, baguettes a beef stew, a variety of cheeses, potatoes with cream cheese and thyme, and a cassoulet served with champagne of course.

"Wow, I can't believe you were so busy today with all the cooking," she said.

"Nah! I just thought I'll make you some different cuisine, I'm good at."

She was so hungry, but could only nibble on all the different foods. They talked for hours, enjoying each moment. After dinner they relaxed in the lounge, discussing music. They both had a love for music in common. The song, Natural High by Bloodstone was playing at the time.

It is so beautiful and serene out there. She got up looking at the view outside. She looked like a princess, not meant for a man to touch. He is staring at the sensual perfection of her face. Her perfume is alluring. Jacques moved towards her. He had to kiss her. As hot as the fire-logs burning in the background, she was filled with flames, the essence of every lust-filled fantasy. She opened her lips to his kiss. The passionate kiss filled her entire system. Her fingers delved through his hair. He kissed her gently on the neck, holding her tight in his strong arms. Jacques's fingers lowered the zipper of her dress. His lips kissed her all over the neck, moving down her jawline.

"You're so pretty, Catherine." he groaned. He pulled her closer by her hips. Jacques laid her down on the soft sofa. His tongue licking over her nipples, his hands stroking, caressing her rounded breasts.

Catherine could feel the overwhelming sensation moving through her entire body. Her body is now yearning with greed, for every touch which filled her with electric pleasure.

She managed to unbutton his shirt. Licking at his nipples, licking all over his chest. Unzipping his pants.

Jacques removed her panties over her hips and his lips move lower down at her thighs. He spread her thighs, kissed her clit, and sucked it until it was swollen. Catherine looked down at Jacques, his face was twisted with pleasure. She grasps her fingers through his hair. He licked and sucked each fold of her pussy and stoke it with his tongue. By now she is squirming with total ecstasy. He parted her lips and pushed his tongue deep inside her, licking the heated liquid coming from her body.

"You taste so sweet, baby!" Jacques growled.

She could barely breathe from all the excitement and elation racing through her. He kissed her again, and sucked at it slowly, so deliciously. She was so close to orgasm. He pulled down his pants and slipped out his thick, hard cock. She could not resist and went down on him. She licked his erected cock which is now dribbling with pre-ejaculation. She pulled the shaft back and lick it slowly, sensually from his balls right up to the tip, he looked down at her pulling her long lustrous hair up.

"Oh God, Catherine, you make me feel so good."

Patience was worn away now. They both worked up a furious, burning tension between them and the need to be inside of each other. He rolled her over on the sofa again. As his tongue reach the entrance of her vagina, licking and teasing her, his tongue plunged deep inside of her. Each penetration of his tongue sends sizzling sensations through her nerve endings. She had multiple orgasms. He slipped his, rock-hard, cock deep inside of her. Her knees gripping his hips with each impalement, deep penetration. The pleasure was exceeding. Each ejaculation, sent repeated, uncontrolled sensations through their bodies. Pure euphoric.

They are finally left limp and exhausted in each other's arms. The past week was heart-rending for her. The pain of dealing with her grief. It was difficult to get over her loss. It was now finally time for her to move on.

"I've never been with anyone since my husband passed on. This was the best. You make me feel so good and whole again." she whispered in his ears.

"Oh my God, Catherine. The feeling is mutual. Could you stay over with me tonight? I want you to be with me all night. I need you." Jacques slid his fingers through her long tresses of hair, he asked from his heart.

"I would love to stay with you Jacques, but I can't. Sundays I spend with my folks. I have lunch there and the family spends the day together, at Mom's." she said hesitantly.

"We did not even touch the dessert, leave some of the desserts for me, and take the rest to your family," Jacques suggested.

"Yeah, that's a good idea. Thank you so much for a lovely evening. It was great." she said.

"When do I see you again, Catherine? I don't even want to let you go. Let me drive behind you, so I know you are safe at home. It's two in the morning, it's rather dangerous on the road."

They both pulled out of the driveway. Catherine knows she's in love. She has this chemistry for him that is written all over her face. It is so apparent. She parked her car in the garage. He got out of his car and kissed her passionately.

"Please don't let me wait long. I can't wait to see you again," he said sadly.

"Okay, tomorrow I'll be back home after six-o-clock. You can come over to my place. Would that be fine with you?" she asked.

"Sure, I'll see you late afternoon around six, thank you, my dear." Jacques kissed her again one more time."

Catherine jumped in the shower. She didn't feel so good in a very long time. She felt safe and cared for. She had a good night's rest and slept peacefully. All excited to see mom and dad the next day.

CHAPTER 2

Early, in the morning she was preparing to go to her family. It's little over half an hour's drive to the North Greenwich side. All she could think of was Jacques. She pulled up in the driveway of her parent's house. As she entered the double-story mansion, walking into the marble foyer, she suddenly thought of Harold, when she introduced him to her parents.

"Hi Mommy, hi Daddy, how are my favorite people in the world? Gosh, I missed you." she greeted and kissed and hugged them tightly.

"Hullo, my dear child. You are very chirpy this morning. And this? Dessert? This is the first time." mom said bewildered.

"What's come over you, my girl?" dad asked.

"I'm good, I'm happy! I had a dinner date last night with a handsome French guy. I will bring him here sometime to meet you. You will love this guy, daddy. He is so kind, gentle, and caring. He even drove behind me last night after dinner, just to see that I'm safe home." she boasted happily.

"Maybe you can invite him for Christmas lunch." dad said.

They always worry about her, especially since her husband passed. She is now twenty-nine years old, but in their eyes, she was their baby. She has three, overprotective brothers and a younger sister. They're all very close.

"We are happy for you, Catherine, just be careful out there. You know you mean the world to us and it's been over a year now. We only want what is best for you." her father's voice rumbled in a warning way.

"Yes Mom, yes Dad, I'm very careful. I'm a big girl, too. I've been married before, it's not like it's my first time. His name is Jacques Dupont. He is a Dentist by trade. His father is French, his mother is Italian. He was married only for a few months and divorced for over five years now. I have known him recently, but it feels like I know him all my life. He helped me the other day, changing my flat tire. I think I'm in love with him, Mom, but we shall take it slow and see how it goes. I promise Mom." she explained to her parents.

"We can't wait to meet him," they said.

Mom was always worried about Catherine's unmarried state.

Lunch on Sundays was a big thing for her mom. Everyone had to dress up. It's like an occasion every week.

"You looking so beautiful, sweetheart. I can see you glowing." her mom turned around and kissed her.

Catherine remembered her years growing up in this strict, protected household. It was a good place to grow up in, though. Her childhood memories. Being raised in a good Christian home, with morals and values. Her brothers and their wives and nieces and nephew all arrived.

"Hey sister, look at you!" they all shouted.

"Looking so glamorous. How have you been, sis?" Richard asked.

"Good, good, I'm all fine, how's everyone?"

They all kissed and hugged. This is how they were raised, in a loving home, with a strong family bond.

"Hey, sweeties. A bear hug for aunty. You all growing so big!" Catherine kissed and squeeze all of them.

Andrea mentioned to Catherine that they needed to do shopping at the boutique, as they had a friend's wedding to attend. It would be a smart affair.

Her sister, Rebecca is the quiet, withdrawn one. She works at a Logistics Company in London. She stays busy and mostly in her own world. Don't socialize much. She sometimes feels a little envious when dad pays too much attention to Catherine, but she loves her sister dearly.

"Why is everyone so noisy today?" Rebecca kissed her sister and the others.

"Your sister met a nice man, Rebecca," said Mom.

"Oh, that's awesome. Why does she get all the good ones, Mom?"

"Don't worry, someday, your other half will walk through that door and sweep you off your feet," Catherine said jokingly.

They embraced their sisterly love.

"Jacques cooked up quite a storm last night, Mom. He better teach me the French cuisine," she said laughing.

Her brothers and everyone were happy for her that she finally, met someone special. Her three sisters-in-law are very close to her and Rebecca. They sometimes, in the past tried to hook Catherine up with their friends. She was very picky though, and never fancied anyone more than a friend. They all had a lovely lunch and the chocolate souffle. Mom made sure that the family gather every week. This is an old family tradition that keeps the family ties alive. It was late afternoon. Family time is over. She greeted everyone, and hold Rebecca tight.

"I see you next week, honey. Be good, I love you lots," she said happily.

She kissed Mom and Dad. She couldn't wait to get to her apartment. She drove home excitedly. She pulled up into her driveway and parked her car in the garage. Jacques was already waiting. Catherine was craving Jacques. Her heart was pounding.

"Is this really happening?" she thought to herself.

"Hullo, love, how was your day?" Jacques greeted her with a kiss, as they walked into the apartment.

"Hi, wonderful, but the day went so long, I couldn't wait to see you. I told them about my new friend. They would like to meet you. They invited you to join us for Christmas lunch. That is if you don't have any other engagements on." she asked politely.

"Thank you, that would be great. I would love to meet all of them. What a beautiful place, Catherine. It's fancy and cozy, just like you. Would you like to go for a drive?" Jacques asked.

"I am a little tired, it's been a long day and it's work tomorrow. Do you mind if I take a raincheck on that drive? We can have a relaxing evening if you are not in a hurry?" she said.

"Oh, yes sure, no problem." Jacques smiled.

"Let me put on some music," she said in a sexy voice.

Her heart and her libido had started revving at the sight of him.

Catherine touched his hair. Stroking her desperate fingers through his thick black hair. He got up. She opened her lips to his kiss. He picked her up and carried her to her bedroom.

"Oh Catherine, I'm so in love with you. I don't want to freak you out. Since the first time, I saw you in the coffee shop. You have captivated my heart, since the moment I laid eyes on you. I have never felt this way before. I've been waiting for you for so long." he whispered in her ear.

Kissing her neck. She wore a one-strap dress, unzipping it from behind, while she lay on top of him, on her big bed. He took off his t-shirt. She lay her head resting on his heart.

"I love you too, Jacques," she said.

While licking her tongue around his nipples. She moved down and smothered his chest with gentle kisses, her hands feathering their way down to his belt. Unzipping his jeans, taking out his hard cock. He crushed her against him, tangling his hand in her hair. She flicked her tongue over his cock, sliding her fingers to his balls. Caressing his balls. Sucking his balls in her mouth. She sucked and stroked him lightly up and down, pulling at his balls and making his dick so hard. He tipped his head back in ecstasy, as pleasure raced through his body, he spilled some in her mouth. He stretched her out on the bed.

Catherine twisted her body until her breasts were pressed against him. His hands ran down her back, hovering over her ass. He slipped the dress down, pulling at the lacy edge of her panty. She lay beside him. He opened her thighs. Kissing her all over. Licking her nipples, cupping her breasts in both hands.

He groaned deeply. "God, I love you."

She needed him so badly. His head moved down, gripping the depths of her pussy. Sucking her clit, she could feel her juices dampening her thighs. He lay on top of her, slow thrust, so hard, fucking her so deep, and intense. She could feel her orgasm building up inside of her. She was losing herself to the pleasure.

"Ah, God, yes, Catherine." His cum squirted inside her.

He had no idea how he managed to have enough breath left in his lungs. They both collapsed elated, on the bed. Looking into each other's eyes. They declared their love for each other. She got up, slipping her silky gown over her bare body.

"You have to go. It's work tomorrow." she smiled.

"Yes, I'll be on my way soon. Let's have coffee. I'll make it. You know Catherine, I've never felt so strongly about anyone before. With you, it's like a special connection. Like I've known you for a long time. The marriage I had was loveless and it was arranged, by my father and his friends. It meant nothing. We were two complete, different personalities. We both agreed to call it quits and it was over in no time. That was when I moved to London and qualified and started my practice. I came here to find love. I have found you, Catherine." he explained.

"Love and reverence go together. When you see the big story, you realize you are in everyone's story and everyone and everything is in yours. Even people you haven't met yet, are part of your story, and you are part of theirs. It was fate, that you should have a flat tire, otherwise we would not have become acquainted. That is love." he added.

She smiles. Always have the, lingering acrimony for the person who is responsible for her husband's death. The reason why she is all alone. The retrospective emotions are killing her well-being. This makes it tremendously difficult to persevere. Sometimes she feels angry that her husband passed away.

She stayed in this grieving process. It's difficult to release some of the pain and suffering associated with the loss.

"I'm trying to find a purpose and meaning in my life. This is part of my healing. I've never felt so good before, as I do now, Jacques. I'm feeling strong feelings for you, too. Knowing someone as special as you are, does wonders, to my healing process. I feel like you are my soulmate. You are giving me a new perspective. I feel like a new person. I'm so happy, I love you, Jacques." she kissed him on the head.

"Let me go." he wrapped his arms around her and kissed her goodnight.

She took a shower and straight to bed. Half an hour later, he sent her a message on her mobile phone.

I am so lucky to have met someone whose presence ignites a burning fire within me. Someone whose infectious smile captures my heart. In an instant, I know the two of us, were meant to be together. I will spend forever, loving you.
Jacques.

She replied.
Together forever, never apart, maybe in distance, but never at heart.

All my love Catherine.

Early Monday morning, it was chilly conditions for parts of Campden. Thundersnow forecast. The news gave warnings of blizzards and high winds. It's two weeks before Christmas and forecasters predict a white Christmas, would be on the cards. Jacques went on a shopping spree, buying gifts for his new love. He bought her chocolates, sexy perfume, and a diamond pendant necklace, with matching earrings. He was excited he could not wait to meet her family.

He booked tickets to go on a cruise ship, after Christmas into the new year. Catherine has beautiful, stylish lounge shirts for gents, at her boutique. She selected the finest ones and some funny neckties for Jacques.

"Good morning, how are you all? So good to see everyone." Catherine greeted.

"We good, how was your weekend? She's smiling, she's smiling." Gary and Albert said.

The girls at work were all happy to see Catherine happy. She deserved it.

"Oh yeah, it was fabulous. My parents invited Jacques for Christmas lunch. They are over the moon, that I have met someone. You know how my parents keep track of my whereabouts. When will I get married, and all their friends have grandchildren. I use to just roll my eyes when I heard that phrase." she said humorously.

The boutique was very busy. It was the busiest time. With the holidays approaching and Christmas. Tourists were hustling down the streets of London. A week before, Catherine put up her little Christmas tree at the start of Advent. It was a cute, small tree. Beautiful green branches. Colorful lights and decorations adorned the tree. She even had empty wrapped-up boxes scattered around. It was Christmas Eve. The two of them exchanged gifts. They kissed under the mistletoe.

She opened her gifts.

"Oh wow, Jacques all these for me? This is so beautiful, oh my God!" she shouted.

"Why are you spoiling me this way? Thank you, thank you, my love," she said excitedly.

"Thank you for my gifts, I love them, too," he said.

The next morning Jacques arrived early at Catherine's place to pick her up to drive to her parents. She was still busy getting ready. As he waited in the lounge for Catherine, he saw pictures of Catherine with her husband who passed. He felt like he saw a ghost. He was in shock. He could not move. He genuinely had no idea, that it was her husband in the accident, he was involved. After the accident, he was quite traumatized.

"Oh my, what am I going to do? She will hate me if she finds out. She would not want to be with me any longer. Even if I should tell her, she would still not want to be with me." Jacques wondered worriedly.

Jacques slipped out by the front door. He got into his car very shaky. He called his brother, Pierre, from his mobile phone. Pierre was busy in the bathroom shaving at the time. His mobile was on speaker phone.

Jacques: Hey, Pierre, how's things.

Pierre: Hi, all good on my side, how are you?

Jacques: I'm fine I guess, but I rather have a difficult situation on my hands right now.

Pierre: Oh no, what's wrong?

Jacques: Remember the accident? The guy who I knocked down and another car drove over him, and he died instantly?

Pierre: Yes, yes, I can remember. It was not your fault, though.

Jacques: He was the husband of the girl, Catherine, whom I'm in love with.

Pierre: Ooh sweet Jesus!

Jacques: I'm at her house to pick her up. We are on our way to her parents, they invited me for lunch.

Pierre: Wow, what an awkward predicament. I'm so sorry for you, brother. Under the circumstances, I don't think you should say anything to her at this stage. It was an accident, remember?

Jacques: Yes, of course. I don't know how she would react if she finds out.

Pierre: Don't worry so much about it, Jacques. Everything will work out fine. Don't spoil anything this time, over Christmas and new year and it is mom's birthday. We all expecting you and Catherine. Keep it quiet, okay! We will sort it out.

Jacques: Yes, thank you, brother. Love you lots. See you soon. Bye.

Pierre: Sure, see you there. Bye.

Pierre was unaware that his devious wife, Savannah was listening in on the whole conversation he had with Jacques. Savannah is conniving and manipulative. She dared to ask Pierre.

"Is everything all right?" expecting him to tell her about Jacques's situation.

"Everything's fine, dear." he sighed.

"All right, I'm ready." Slipping her fur mink over her red, velvet dress. Her father bought her and Rebecca the same mink coats, last Christmas.

She noticed he came from outside.

"Is everything okay with you? You're looking rather pale. If you not feeling well, we can do this another day."

"No, I'm fine. We can leave. You look so beautiful Catherine."

"Some patient called, she said her dentures broke, she needed it fixed urgently. I explained to her that we are closed for the holidays, and what the name of the product was, and she could purchase it at the pharmacy. All is well, let's go."

He opened the door of his sporty BMW, and she smiles.

"I feel like a queen." she kissed him on the lips.

The drive was long. Jacques felt very tense and uneasy in the car. Catherine could sense something is not right.

"You're very quiet, Jacques. Are you nervous about meeting my parents? They are very calm and polite, but firm as well. You will love them, I promise you." she said.

"I'm sure I will. Talking about parents, are you ready to meet mine, Catherine?"

"Oh yes, of course, any time," she added excitedly.

"So, after Christmas day, we will be going on a cruise liner for a couple of days. We are going on the Anthem of the Seas, from London to Paris. We shall be back around the first day of January. My mom's 60th birthday bash is the next day. You have to pack your suitcases tonight."

"Ooh my dear Jacques, that will be awesome. Thank you, sweetheart," she said delightfully.

Jacques smiled at her squeezing her hand.

"We five minutes away," he said.

Everyone arrived, by the time they pulled up.

Dad was busy upstairs dressing. He pushed his tie between

the top buttons of his white, vigorously ironed shirt and carefully rolled up his sleeves. Inwards, onefold at a time. He is such a perfectionist. He heard a car pull up and stared out the window. Looking handsome in his formal attire. He saw Jacques open the door for Catherine.

"Oh, what a gentleman. That's what I admire in a man," he told himself.

He quickly came down the stairs. Mom was busy in the kitchen with the final preparations for lunch.

"Hello, everybody. I would like to introduce to you, Jacques Dupont," she said happily.

"Jacques, meet my father, James Darcy, my mother Jemima, sister Rebecca, and my brothers, Colin, Richard, and Miles. Their wives, Olivia, Andrea, and Sophia. My nieces, Abigail and Annabelle, and nephew Ethan. They are my pride and joy." she added.

"Hi, I'm so pleased to meet all of you. You seem like a tight family." Jacques shook hands and was full of smiles with all of them.

"Come give me a hug." Mom grabbed him and gave him a tight hug.

"Mm, you smell so good, what a lovely person. So nice to meet you. Welcome to the family." her mother said all excitedly.

"So now I understand why my daughter has all these sparkles in her eyes and she is glowing. She has child-bearing hips. Gosh, I can't wait to have more grandchildren." she said.

"Mom, you embarrassing me." Catherine rolled her eyes, looking at dad.

Jacques laughed.

"He is a real catch, Rebecca thought to herself. I wonder if he has a brother."

They soon settled in at the dining room table.

"I heard you in the dentistry, Jacques." her father confirmed.

"Yes, after I qualified, I moved to London. My family is in Paris. I have two brothers and one sister. My mother is a retired teacher and my father has his own perfume company. My brothers are running the company."

"Catherine, can you please help me in the kitchen, love?" mom called.

"Sure, mom. Becca, let's go!" Catherine chuckled.

"Wow, look at that beautiful jewelry, my child. You know Catherine, when a man gives a woman, diamonds, that is for keeps. Diamonds are forever. Please hold on to him, don't you mess up, and that's an order. I would love to have him as a son. You not getting any younger, my dear. Your biological clock is ticking." mom warned.

"Yes mom, we taking it slow I don't want to rush into things. We only starting now and getting to know each other. I do feel very strongly about him, mom. I think I'm in love. I'm just so scared of getting hurt. I cannot handle any more pain, as I already suffered from the loss of Harold." she said softly in a weepy voice.

"Awe man, Rebecca holding her tight. Don't feel so weary, Catherine. You know you are really lucky to have someone so sweet and gentle. He is gorgeous. He can't keep his eyes off you, Catherine. Everything will work out fine, you'll see. We'll make him feel extra special." Rebecca, assured.

"Now wipe those tears and help your sister set the table," Mom ordered.

While the girls setting the table, the guys were chatting away.

"Maybe this year, more than others, we can appreciate being able to gather around the table to celebrate our friends and family this Christmas. Last year the sons and their families were abroad. It was only a few of us. Today my home is full. We are happy that you are our guest today, Jacques." dad said.

Mom took out crisp red and white table linens, cozy candles, fine crystal glasses, and cutlery. Rebecca did the origami napkin work and some embroidered napkins from grandma. She did it the night before. Crackers were added to the table.

CHAPTER 3

Laughter and joy filled the house. The atmosphere was joyous. The little terrors played around. There was a huge Christmas tree, with beautiful decorations, in the lounge area. Lots of gifts for everyone.

Lunch was served.

"Everyone seated?" dad asked.

"Let's pray."

'Dear Loving Father, thank you Lord for being the Prince of Peace, and I ask you that supernatural peace reign in our hearts.

Blessed is the season which engages the whole world in a conspiracy of Love. Thank you for my family and our new guest today. May we eat this food with humbleness in our hearts and be forever grateful, in Jesus' name, Amen.'

Richard got up. "I'd like to drink a toast."

'May we all have the gladness of Christmas which is hope. The spirit of Christmas which is peace. The heart of Christmas which is love.

Especially to our dearest sister Catherine and Jacques, may your love grow from now until eternity. Blessed Christmas everyone.'

"Thank you, he smiled. This means so much to me. I'm lucky to be part of this family. I feel honored to be a guest in your beautiful home with beautiful people. Thank you, everyone." Jacques said.

They all had a lovely time eating all kinds of different foods and desserts on the menu. The ladies also brought different treats along. Families and friends popped in for the festive spirit. Jacques was loving the gathering so much, that he forgot all about the accident issue.

By late afternoon, Catherine got up and tapped a spoon against a glass.

"Can I get everybody's attention, please?" she asked.

"Jacques and I will be leaving tomorrow on a cruise ship. We will be away for a few days. After the new year, I will meet his family. Isn't this fabulous? I'm so excited, I can't wait. I have some packing to do. Jacques only told me this, on our way here. I'm going to love and leave you all."

"Oh lovely, that is so fantastic. You guys must have a wonderful time. Be safe and take care of each other. Keep in touch." her dad said.

"You must all enjoy the rest of the day." she greeted and hugged everyone.

Jacques thanked all of them for a glorious Christmas day he thoroughly enjoyed.

They drove off back to Catherine's place.

"What a pleasure to have met your family. I'm happy you brought me here, Catherine."

"I'm happy too. Now for the next hurdle. I hope your parents will like me."

"I'm certain they will. They are very kind and soft people. They looking forward to meeting you, too."

After Jacques dropped her off, she took a drive up to the boutique to get some gifts for Jacques's parents. Then she packed her suitcases.

The next morning, he picked her up and loaded the suitcases in the boot of his car. His friend and cycling buddy, Micah was also sitting in the back seat. She opened the door of the car and nodded at the guy.

"Hi I'm Micah, please to meet you."

She greeted Micah.

"He is dropping us at the harbor. My car will be parking in his garage. We have to be at the port early."

Arriving at the harbor, they greeted Micah, unloaded the suitcases, and embarked on the cruise ship. They entered the terminal. The check-in process can be overwhelming and chaotic, especially at that time of the year, but they generally are organized. The cruise line staff directed them to their appropriate line, the high-status suite passengers.

As they settled in their beautiful suite, they took a stroll on the ship to see what excursions, activities, and a variety of onboard attractions there were. On a cruise ship, you have to dress up for dinner.

A while later, the ship was full. All the passengers were settled.

"All aboard!" called the captain.

The ship started to sail. It was the most beautiful sight. Catherine had a little seasickness, but that passed, as soon as they got the fresh air from the oceans. Jacques wanted to do some activities on the cruise. They went to a variety of Broadway shows and themed deck parties. Lots of eating throughout the day. After dinner, they watched the beautiful sunset. His gazing over the oceans, at the stars, was so romantic. The waves waltz along the seashore, going up and down in gentle rhythms. She started having burning cravings for Jacques, as his fingertips stroked down her arms. A big gush of wind swept through the top deck of the cruise liner. He stood behind her, holding her tight. He could not resist her smell, kissing her neck from behind. She could feel his cock growing harder behind her. With the hunger of his touch and his arousal, she wanted him right there. She wore a short mini dress with red high heel shoes. There was a party on the deck, but Jacques wanted to make love to her, instead. They went back to their suite. The room was light and dim and they could hear the sounds of the waves splashing against the ship. He laid her down on the bed and continue to kiss her on her neck, behind her ears. "Hmm, I can feel your warm breath and it's driving me crazy," she whispered.

Her breathing accelerated as he circled his tongue around her nipples.

"Tell me what you need, baby." he urged.

While moving down, opening her thighs, kissing her, caressing, each stroke of his tongue, his lips sending a blazing fire through her body. It was pure ecstasy. He needed to fuck her right now. He deep thrust his tongue in her pussy. He groaned and lick the glistening liquid from her lips. She grabbed him while laying on her back, with his knees beside her face, sucking his cock. From his balls up to the tip, she licked until he spilled some in her face. He lay on top of her penetrating her with all his might until he slumped on the bed.

"Awe Catherine, you make me feel so good. I love you so much," he said.

He lay beside her, keeping his face on her chest. Some worry always gets the better of him. The worry of he might lose her.

"Catherine, I want you to know that I love you with all my heart and soul. Whatever happens, I never want to lose you," he said.

"Never, I love you more. I'm here to stay. My love for you will never die." she assured.

They went out to have a bite to eat and just sit around listening to the jazz band at one of the many attractions. Then to the next. This went on right through the night, every night. Some days they went out to do the activities. There wasn't much time to sleep. Catherine called her mom every day and told her about all the fun they had on the ship and how beautiful it was. She sent them pictures of her and Jacques, on the beautiful vessel, with the oceans in the background.

The next day was New Year's eve. They have a ball for the evening. Catherine wearing her emerald ballroom gown, with off shoulders. She looked exquisitely beautiful. He wore one of the lounge shirts she gave him with a bowtie and black pants. He kissed her passionately. He could never resist her. Tonight, she looked extraordinarily beautiful. Just before they had to leave for the ball and dinner extravaganza, Jacques wanted them to stay at the suite. He did not want to lose out, on one moment alone with her. This is a special kind of passionate love. Catherine insisted, that she won't want to miss out on all the festivities.

They went to dinner on the lower deck to be part of the celebrations. Everyone was dressed up elegantly. All the people danced to the music playing. It was time for the final countdown to the New Year. The beautiful displays of the fireworks, glazed in the night sky. Everyone shouted, Happy New Year!

Jacques kissed her and made a wish.

"Happy New Year, my love."

The party went on the whole night. In the early hours of the morning, after breakfast, the cruise liner docked at Paris harbor. Port Quai de Grenelle is located on the banks of the Seine River. The Eiffel tower is not far from there. First, they had to take forty-five minutes, to drive to his parents' home. There were mini-cabs parking at the port for passengers to be transported to their relevant destinations. The driver loaded the luggage in the cab and off they drove to the very upmarket area, Saint-Germaine-des -Pres. It's time to meet the family.

"They expecting us, I'm so excited." Jacques grinned.

"Wow, look at this place? I've never been to Paris before. Breathtaking!"

She was nervously fiddling with her fingers, as the arrival of his parents' house got closer. Catherine is a smart elegant girl, who dresses for success. Suddenly she wondered if she looked fine. First impressions are always important. She felt apprehensive. Her heart is pounding.

"And we're here," Jacques said with a smile.

They pulled up in this huge driveway, big enough for ten cars.

"We going to be fine. You looking pretty."

As they entered the house, she received a warm welcome from his mom and dad. Her anxiety vanished and she was calm and relaxed. She needed to let them know that she, appreciate their time and would like to reciprocate in kindness.

"Bonjour! Mom, Dad, so good to see you." Jacques shook hands with his father, air-kissed both sides of his face, and hugged tightly. He lifted mom, hugged her for a moment, and kissed her five times, ten times or more.

"Happy New Year!!" he shouted.

"Gosh, I missed you guys. Meet my girlfriend, Catherine Darcy. This is my mother Genevieve and dad Francois Dupont.

"Mademoiselle, Monsieur, I'm so honored to meet you."

"The pleasure is ours." they both replied.

"Awe, it's so nice to see you, my son." Mom's eyes filled with tears.

"It's been a long time, Jacques." dad growled.

"Come let's have cake and tea." mom said.

"I got you both some gifts. I have a boutique in London, I hope you will like it, Monsieur," she said

"Oh no, don't call me Monsieur, Uncle Franc, and Aunty Gene, is good." dad chuckled.

"Could I help you in the kitchen, Aunty Gene?" Catherine asked eagerly.

"Yes, please do. I wanted to talk to you about Jacques."

She followed Aunty Gene down the long passage to the kitchen.

"You have a beautiful home, Aunty, so massive."

"Yes, thank you, my dear. There is a guest room for you, down the hallway, and Jacques's room, stays empty since he left. Jacques is the youngest of the boys. He is a very soft and gentle man. You know a few years ago, his father arranged for him to get married. For heaven's sake, it only lasted a few months. I never agreed to it, as I know my son. But his dad always thought that he knows what is best for his children. It was obvious, that they'd never been together. She was a nice girl, but they were no match for each other. I know my Jacques. He knows what quality he looks for in a woman. I asked them to annul the marriage." Gene explained.

"What about you, I can see the happiness in Jacques's eyes," she said happily.

Catherine pushes her hair away from her eyes, concerned about what she is told about Jacques.

"We only met recently. He is a real, kind-hearted, gentleman. We spent Christmas with my family. They adored him. We have strong feelings for each other. I've been married, my husband passed away, almost a year ago. We never started a family. It's been tough for me. Since I met Jacques, I feel like a brand, new person." Catherine said.

"That is so sad. You see, my girl, the moment I saw you, I could see that you and Jacques are meant for each other. I'm his mother, I know him." Franc and Jacques could be heard chatting away from the lounge area.

"Jacques, how're things going at work? We haven't heard from you in a while, until last week. You know your mother always worries about you." dad complained.

"It's very busy at the surgery, dad."

He laid across the small sofa, legs hanging over it. There was never room for his long limbs. This was his favorite spot.

"We going to check into a hotel, later this afternoon."

"Are you serious? No ways. We have enough room here.

Your mom will have no such thing. Don't upset your mother now. You just got here. This is a fine, young lady. Stay with us. Your brothers will be here any minute now. They took the kids to watch the fireworks display. Angel is away. She went camping with her friends, but she'll be back tonight."

Minutes later, they all arrived. Jacques jumped up to greet his brothers.

"Hey, hey stranger! Good to see you!!" they slapped each other behind their backs as they hugged.

Arthur's wife, Juliette, and Savannah brought the kids inside. The kids ran in and out again to go play.

"Go greet Meme and Pepe," shouted Juliette.

The kids greeted quickly and ran out fast again, to go play. Outside is a big play park area, with swings and jungle gyms. They love the trampoline.

"Bonjour, Beau. How are you all doing? Nice to see you, Jacques. You are very scarce." Juliette said.

They could hear giggling coming from the kitchen, as they walked down the passage. Then there was a great burst out of laughter. Gene was cracking a joke about Jacques's love for cooking and that Catherine should learn to do French cuisine, the way to his heart.

This was when Savannah and Juliette walked into the kitchen.

"Hi, Catherine, nice to finally meet you. We've heard so much about you. All good things, though." Juliette smiled.

Catherine smiled and shook hands with her. Savannah just nodded her head, in an antisocial manner. She refused to take Catherine's hand.

"Pleased to meet you too, Savannah," Catherine said.

Juliette was a friendly, kind lady. She was loved by everyone. They have been married for eight years. Arthur and Juliette have a good stable marriage. Pierre on the other hand, have a troublesome marriage. His wife Savannah, was very controlling over him. She had an attitude problem. This was not difficult for Catherine to pick up. She could sense it when Savannah walked into the kitchen. Savannah had that threatening, unfriendly look on her face, like, this is her territory. Her character was written all over her face.

They all walked to the lounge, where all the men were congregating. They were all laughing and having fun. Savannah felt uncomfortable. Like she didn't belong there. Arthur and Pierre greeted Catherine.

"Aha! She's a real catch, isn't she? Loads of style. She's very beautiful. You've done it this time Jacques." Pierre said.

Savannah stood by the side of the table. She gazed at Pierre, with those looks that could kill. It was like feeding the devil. Criticism was particularly prevalent, in Savannah. Her facial expressions and body language said it all. She tried to put a fake smile on her face. They all know her so well.

"So how long have you and Jacques known each other, Catherine? It wasn't after several months when Pierre brought me here to meet the family." Savannah said sarcastically.

Savannah was annoying everyone around her. Catherine just stared at her and laughed. She did not take offense.

Arthur looked at Jacques. There was something he wanted to talk to him about. Like was there any hope that he might do something in terms of their mother and father? If he could come, more often to see them, even for short visits. It would mean so much to them and take so little out of him. London is only a little over an hour's flight to see his parents. It would also lift a great deal of the burden off Arthur and Pierre's backs. Jacques was the youngest of the three sons. He would have to talk to him sometime, somewhere private.

Juliette and Angel organized Gene's 60th birthday bash. The atmosphere became a little tense, after Savannah's stupid remarks. Juliette broke the ice.

"Let's check all the final details about the party." she smiled at them all in good humor again.

The Theme is 'Vegas Nights.'

"I have everything sorted. The caterers, the venue, and the guest list. Angel sorted the flowers and the menu out. Angel sorted almost everything out by herself." Juliette confirmed and shout with delight.

Savannah had, like a permanent shrewd face. She was always ready for an argument, or put anyone in their place and always wanted to have her way. For no apparent reason, or maybe because Catherine is around, she's been more miserable. It was early in the evening. Everyone left.

"We are going for a night out in the town. I have to take her to the Eiffel Tower." Jacques mentioned.

"We'll get ready and wait for Angel to come."

"Franc, have you noticed a bleak look on Jacques' face? I see dark rings around his eyes, apart from him being happy with Catherine. I always worry about my boy. Moms always know best, and I am certain something is worrying him." she told her husband.

"Oh, how so? I haven't noticed anything. I think he seems pretty happy to me. I think he found his match. Catherine is a real grand girl. You think something is driving him?" Franc asked concerningly.

"Apart from Savannah's absurd remarks, something worries him. We'll have to ask him, but let's leave it for after the party." Gene suggested.

"Yes, you're right. We don't want to spoil your birthday vibe." Franc kissed her and embraced her tight.

"I love you, Gene, you are the best, you are my rock. I don't know what I'll do without you," he said.

At that moment, Jacques and Catherine walked in and saw them embracing and kissing.

"Awe, that is so cute, so sweet. When you see this, you just know that this is the purest form of love, you can find on this earth. First, our parents gave us our life, but then they try to give us their life." Catherine exclaimed.

A car pulled up outside, very noisily. It was Angel arriving from her camping trip at La Roche Posay.

"Bonjour! Everybody. Aah, it's so good to be back home. Boy, I'm tired, she sighed!" She wrapped her arms around mom and dad and of course her brother she hadn't seen in months.

"My dear, brother. It's been so long. Oh, my gosh. This must be Catherine. Wow, what an exquisitely, beautiful young woman. I'm so happy to meet you. I'm Angelique, they call me Angel around here." she laughed.

"Thank you, nice meeting you too, Angel." she smiled.

"You on your way out? We must do something together, soon." she babbled excitedly.

"Yes, we going around town, some sightseeing to do," Jacques concluded.

"All right, I need to take a shower and I desperately need my bed. Be safe and enjoy. See you tomorrow. It's party time." she yelled.

Jacques was about to call a cab when his father stopped him.

"Don't be foolish, how can you take a girl out sightseeing, in a cab. Here are my keys. Take my car." his father insisted vehemently.

"Thanks, Dad," he replied.

"You have an awesome family, Jacques. Your parents are the most loving. Ah, and Angel, she's like a real angel...I love her." she spoke softly and wrap her arms around him and kissed him lightly. Jacques seemed distant and a little uneasy.

"Your brothers are also very nice and Juliette. As for Savannah, she's quite a character," she murmured.

"Yes, she can be very wicked. That is her nature. You'll soon see her weird ways." he relented.

"Are you okay, Jacques? You've been mighty quiet, lately."

"Of course, I'm good," Jacques assured her.

"I must take you to The Louvre Museum. It's the most beautiful, historical museum in the world. It is the home of work of some of the best-known works of art, including the Mona Lisa and the Venus de Milo. But there we have to go another day. Spend lots of time there. Let's stop at the Eiffel Tower. Lots of gardens to picnic under the Tower."

They walked to the first level at the Atrium of the Pavilion Ferrie.

"This is the most beautiful city, the canals, incredible sights, gastronomic atmosphere. It brings out the romantic vibe," she emphasized.

"Oh wow, this is too beautiful for words," she said surprisingly.

'Catherine Darcy, I declare my love for you. If my love were an ocean, there would be no more land. If my love were a desert, you would only see sand. If my love were a star, there would only be light. I love you always and forever, Jacques Dupont'

He wrote on the hearts of *#EiffelinLove*.

"Your turn, Catherine," he whispered.

'Jacques Dupont, when I look into your eyes, I know I have found the mirror of my soul. I declare my undying love to you. We are mutual in divine love, Catherine Darcy'

They kissed passionately. What more beautiful memory could there be, than seeing the declaration of their love posted on the Eiffel Tower. They took pictures.

"This is my highlight of Paris. I shall treasure this, forever. I'm so mesmerized by this place. Let's go to the next level. There's a gift store up there. I want to buy Angel a pretty gift." she said.

Hand in hand they walked their way up the steps to the second level. Catherine took out a cute bracelet.

She walked to the other side of the boutique and found a lovely jacket.

"You think she will like this, Jacques?"

"I suppose so, if you like it, she will too, I'm sure," Jacques replied.

"Let me take the jacket and the bracelet."

She asked the lady if she could have the gift, wrapped up.

"Thank you so much, Mademoiselle."

"You're welcome." she smiled.

Still strolling around, the two lovers, admire the view. They moved up to the next level, the Champagne Bar. Jacques grew up in Paris. He visited around there and picnicked with his family when he and his brothers were kids. He never realized the significance of going into the Eiffel Tower. Only now he perceived, being with the love of his life. They sat there for hours taking in the breathtaking views. Talking, looking into each, other's eyes. They're very much in love.

"Catherine, I just want you to know that, whatever happens, just remember I will love you forever."

Jacques swept her long silky hair to the back. He placed his hands cupping her face and kissed her gently. French kissing, holding her tight, on the top level of the Eiffel Tower. How romantic. She kissed him right back.

"I love you too, my dear," she whispered in his ear.

He held her in his arms from behind and kissed her. He just couldn't get enough of this woman. It was after midnight, but very busy with lots of loving couples hanging around.

"It's getting late, we have to get back. We have to be up early in the morning," she said.

"Yes, we can go now."

They made their way down the tower, hand in hand, lovingly, kissing every moment they can. They weren't going to stay out all night, as the next day was going to be very busy. But when you're there, you could not resist.

"We must come back here, real soon. This city is super awesome, a place full of love on every corner, most beautiful scenery. I could stay here forever." Catherine told Jacques.

"This is the best night of my life, Catherine. I feel so happy, I don't want it to end." he proposed.

"No ways, this is only the beginning," she assured.

Jacques pulled up and parked his father's car in the garage.

"We have to be very, quiet. I don't want to wake them," she whispered. She went into the guest room, which Aunty Gene showed her earlier that evening. They kissed goodnight. Jacques settled in his old room. He felt restless. He tossed and turned. He struggled to fall asleep. He needed Catherine.

A short while later, Catherine's shiny, long black hair was piled on top of her head in a messy bun. After undressing, she slipped over only her silky gown. She just needed to check in her suitcase for the outfit to wear for the birthday party, before taking a shower. She bent over to take the dress out. Jacques slipped in quietly, without her noticing. As she looked up, startled at first, then bewildered. He gave her a lascivious wink.

CHAPTER 4

"What are you doing here?" she demanded. Her frown deepened.

"This is your parents' home they are just down the hallway way. You cannot be here, Jacques," she mumbled softly.

He could not resist her curves shining through her silky gown under the moonlight shadows, glancing through the window. He kissed her. She couldn't resist him either. He had to have her, even just for a quick moment. He wanted to make love to her all night. Her nightgown slipped off. She was naked. He kissed her neck and ravished her all over. His hands over her breasts, sucking her nipples, right down on his knees he went. He licked her, sucking all her juices. She was all worked up and burning with desire. She rubbed and pressed her pussy against his raging hard-on which he was sporting beneath his silk boxers. His cock was so very hard and erected, that she pulled down his boxers. Her hands roved over his chest. She licked his nipples. Her beautiful fingers wrapped around his cock and she put him in her mouth. His mind screamed at him to take her, and he penetrated her in a standing position, against the wall. Lifting her, with her legs wrapped around his hips, he thrust her. For a few seconds, he thought he was going to shoot his load right there. The built-up craving for her all night. He needed this. He quietly, tip-toed out of the room.

The following morning, everyone was up early. Catherine handed Angel her gift.

"For me? Awe merci, merci. You're so sweet. Thank you, sweetheart!"

Jacques, Catherine, and Angel went into the room and sang happy birthday to their mom Gene and she woke up. Francois also chorused and smiled.

"Merci, merci, my lovely children. Let's all sit outside on the porch and have some coffee, buns, and croissants."

They grabbed her and gave her a bear hug, then dad closed the love blanket.

"We love you mom, more than you will ever know," they emphasized.

"Thank you, Catherine, for the lovely gifts. We love it. Thanks so much." Gene said.

"It's my pleasure, aunty. I'm glad you like it."

"Looking forward to the bash, Mom? How many people have you invited? We leave early tomorrow morning, but I promise I will be visiting more often, at least once a month." Jacques reassured her.

"Well, you have to ask your sister, not too many I guess, around sixty guests. Your aunties and uncles from both sides, all the immediate family and some close friends. Your Aunty Rosalie came from Italy." she confirmed.

"I would love that. That would be awesome. I would love to see more of you. And do bring Catherine with, you anytime." mom answered.

It was a cold day as usual, with little sun rays bursting through the clouds. They got up after three hours, enjoying the late morning unwinding. Bonding with her children meant the world to her. She remained to have a close relationship with all her children.

Late afternoon, they all dressed up for the sensational event. They drove to the lavish venue 'Renaissance Paris Arc de Triomphe Hotel.'

"We'll drive with Angel in her SUV, dad. We see you there."

The birthday girl wore a beautiful silver sequin, chiffon, maxi dress with long flowing sleeves. Angel styled her hair in soft curls, with a matching sequin band. Her husband had on a black tuxedo and a bowtie. They all arrived at the glamorous affair. As they walked in at the entrance, there was a red carpet. The theme is the 'Vegas Nights' Casino party. Lighting décor greeted them as they entered the entranceway. Huge, aluminum inflated balloons, featured a mixture of Hearts, Diamond, and Spades in a big white, red and black, Happy 60th Birthday banner. The music played. The era of music, when Genevieve was a young girl in the 1960s. She looked very youthful. Juliette and Angel organized a concierge service at your side.

"I picked all the décor and flowers. Mom loves diamonds." Angel told Catherine.

The tables were set in black, white, and silver, with a white rhinestone accent. Crystal candelabra adorn each table. On the menu would be, Caviar and lobsters, seafood platters, and edible silver leaf served, alongside champagne cocktails on ice and bubbly non-alcoholic refreshments. On the one side, there was an area where all the gifts piled up. All the guests arrived in groups. Arthur and Juliette were already there with little Zoe. She looked like a little flower girl, with her dark pink stiffening frock and diamante pumps.

Gene sat in her special chair at the Custom Table Centerpiece. As the guests walked in, they all wished her happy birthday. On one side there was a Collage of all her pictures as a baby, school going, college, wedding pictures, and when she had her children. This was just awesome.

"Where is Pierre? How can he be late for his mother's celebration?" Angel asked.

Pierre was late. He only arrived one hour after the party started.

He and Savannah and their two boys, Lois and Jules walked in. Francois could see there was trouble in Little China, again.

"Pierre, could I have a word with you please?"

"Yes dad, we argued. Savannah always seems to have a problem with anything. I'm so sorry dad." he answered.

It was like he knew his father was very upset.

"Please keep it civil. Don't cause a scene here tonight. All the family is around. Please don't humiliate your mother. People like to gossip." dad gave him a stern warning.

On the other side of the hall were buffet tables set with decadence. All different kinds of cakes and desserts, assorted waffles and teas and coffees. Savannah kept to herself, mingling with family members. It was time for a toast. Juliette was already standing by Gene. Dad called up Arthur, Pierre, and Jacques.

"Come, Catherine, let's go up," Angel called.

"My dear Genevieve, you entered your sixth decade. I've

never met anyone with more enthusiasm for life. You are an inspiration to all of us. It's my honor to be your husband. I love you, and I thank you all." dad toasted.

Arthur took the mike from his father.

"I'd like to make a toast from all of us.

You shine brighter and better than the sunshine after days of thunderstorms. You are even better than that ray of hope after long periods of despair. Who are you? You are the best mom ever. Happy Birthday, Mom. We love you!"

"Thank you, thank you." mom said tearfully.

"Let's have a photoshoot everybody."

"Anyone wants to have their pictures taken with the birthday girl, please do come up on the stage, and enjoy the evening." dad announced.

People ate, socialized, and danced the night away. Families who didn't see each other for ages. Arthur and Jacques went outside for a smoke.

"How're things, Jacques? You leaving tomorrow morning, I believe." Arthur asked.

"Yeah, but I told mom I'll try to come to visit them at least once a month. I promised them." Jacques said to his brother.

"I was planning to have a talk to you regarding them, but you have confirmed it yourself now," Arthur said.

"Good, brother. We will appreciate that, and we all miss you too, so that would be great. And before I forget, Catherine is a lovely girl." Arthur said smiling.

"Thank you. I give you, my word." Jacques promised.

Pierre's boys were dressed in cute suites, with waistcoats. They were running around with their cousins. He kept an eye on them. Jacques and Arthur came in from outside.

At the tables Catherine and Angel were babbling away, eating and enjoying themselves.

"I finished my bachelor of law program. It's called 'License de Droit' here in Paris. At first, I wanted to do modeling. Then I changed my mind. I'm done with my, two years Master of Law program LLM. Last year I completed my J.D and graduated. I qualified as an advocate. My dad wanted me to join the company, but I suppose I'm like Jacques. We had our interests at heart. My dad is quite fragile. Arthur is the CEO and Pierre is the managing director of the perfume company. Savannah also works in the sales department. I do have an interest in the company. I love parfums. I just wanted to do something differently." Angel explained.

"That is so awesome. You must come to visit us in London. Stay for some time, whenever you are free. I would love to have you there. In February we have a catwalk show in Milan. Competition with all the designers. I will inform you about that." Catherine proposed.

"That would be great. I need a break."

Jacques's eyes fell on Catherine. He was delighted when he saw his sister and Catherine getting along so well.

"You look so beautiful tonight, my love. I could just eat you up." Jacques whispered in her ear.

"Let me go to the ladies' room." she giggled.

"When you come back, we should have a dance, okay?" Jacques ordered.

He sat at the table with Angel. They worried about Pierre looking so gloomy.

"Catherine is a real cutie, smart, elegant girl. You make a lovely couple. I like her. I like her a lot, Jacques." Angel, approved.

"Thanks, sweetie. What's with Pierre? He's been downhearted all night." Jacques asked.

"It must be his wife, of course," she confirmed.

Jacques stood up and greeted his aunties and uncles as he walked his way over to Pierre.

"Hey, what's up bro?" Jacques asked.

"It's work issues. Savannah wants me to sign over my shares of the company in her name. She wants to have a higher position in the company. Dad would never allow this. She threatens to leave me and take the boys with her. She stressing me out, this woman." he complained.

"How're things on your side, Jacques? I hear you leaving tomorrow morning."

"Yeah, but I will be around, more often." he gave his word.

"Yes, dad's health is not so good anymore. He gets tired and fatigued more regularly, recently. Savannah became more troublesome, whenever I go to mom, she protests. She would ask, why can't Arthur do it? She drives me insane, that woman. Oh, and the issue with Catherine's husband. We have to think of how to work around that situation. Maybe you should just tell her about it, I'm sure she'd understand. It was an accident." Pierre looked at him helplessly.

"I guess I have to cross that bridge when the time is right," he suggested.

As Catherine walked to the restrooms, she was astonished at what she saw. There was Savannah, her dress lifted. The guy's pants pulled down, and they were making out in one of the cloakrooms, close to the restrooms. The guy was Jacques's cousin's husband. She turned around and stopped in her tracks to take a full glance.

"Is this true?" she thought to herself.

Savannah looked at her in shock. Catherine wasn't too sure if it was more a state of shock or guilt. This woman had no dignity.

Catherine looked at her with a wry look on her face, then she shook her head in shame and walked on.

When Catherine walked towards the tables, Jacques's aunties were busy talking to Angel and Jacques.

The aunties waved at Catherine. She greeted them. They continued their discussions with Angel about her graduation and the advocacy trade.

Catherine glanced around and saw Savannah walking around innocently.

"Where are Lois and Jules?"

Lois was Savannah and Pierre's six-year-old son, just freshly started Grade 1. Jules is at Pre-school.

"They with the nanny," answered Pierre, as he sat down with them at the table.

"You have a nanny? What do they do?"

The words slipped out before Catherine could call them back, and she blushed when she realized what she'd said. She'd assumed that Savannah is capable of raising her kids. Most mothers do.

Catherine felt a little uneasy and called Angel from the opposite side of the table to have something to eat with her. They dug into the caviar with lobsters and sushi rolls.

Slow jams of the 60's music played. Songs like, 'Hello Stranger' by Barbara Lewis, 'Hey there Lonely Girl, and songs by Stylistics, Dramatics, and various other artists.

Jacques fluttered his eyes at her, for a dance, she had promised. She nodded her head at him and smiled. He took her hand and walk towards the dance floor. She wore a dress that talked about her personality and everyone's eyes stayed on her. A long, full black sequin, evening gown, with an open back. She looked like a million dollars. Her lips whispered incantations. She created the impression that he was leading her. They were dancing the night away.

"I could hold you in my arms like this all night," Jacques said softly in her ear.

One could see the despised look in Savannah's eyes when she looked at Catherine. The dance floor was hustling with couples dancing. Francois and Gene were dancing in the center and everyone else formed a circle around them, cheering them. A few couples on the dance floor promenaded randomly. It was great fun and laughter all the way. Sometime during a dance break, Catherine passed Savannah, on their way to the waffle station. She touches the tips of her thumb and the index finger and slides them over her closed mouth in a gesture, my lips are sealed. Your secret is safe with me. If looks could kill. They glanced at one another with deep abomination.

The dancing and eating continued until late hours, close to midnight.

Juliette tapped a spoon against a glass to draw everyone's attention.

"Hey everyone, Gene has a speech to make."

Gene took the mike from Juliette.

"So, we've come to the end of my birthday celebration. I would like to take this opportunity, to thank everybody for spending my special night with me, and also to all the organizers and caterers. Everything was just perfect. I want to thank you all in abundance for everyone's presence. I hope you all had a spectacular time. Please feel free to take some eatables with you on your way out. There are containers for you to put the goodies in. Thank you, once again. I had a lovely evening." she announced.

Soon the guests greeted and left, in groups as they arrived earlier in the evening. The last ones were the immediate family.

"Thank you for all your hard work. You did an excellent job and your delicious foods made our event special." Francois recounted.

Pierre carried Jules to the car, and Laura, the nanny was already sitting with Lois, fast asleep in the back seat of his car. Savannah left without greeting. Pierre ran back inside, to say his goodbyes to Jacques and Catherine.

"Brother Jacques, I'll be seeing you soon."

They shook hands and embrace. He hugged Catherine as well.

"We'll be in contact. Au revoir!"

"Definitely, for sure. Keep well. Take care. Au revoir."

Pierre greeted everyone else. Juliette and Arthur were also on their way home and greeted Jacques and Catherine.

"Your brother is such a sweet, soft, and gentle man. That deceitful woman doesn't deserve him." Catherine testified.

They all drove home in the SUV.

"What time will you be leaving?" Angel asked.

"Around 6 am. All our suitcases are ready. Dad will drop us at the airport."

They pulled up into the driveway and parked the car in the garage. They arrived home before their parents.

"All right, so I guess I should also greet you guys. Catherine, it's been awesome to have met you. Thank you for the time we've spent together. And thank you for my lovely gifts. Please do come soon, and I will come to visit you. Take care of my brother. He needs someone like you." she kissed and hugged Catherine.

"Jacques, you know you are my favorite. You be good and take care of each other. I love you dearly." she held him for a moment.

"Yarning, I have to hit the sack now. I can't keep my eyes open. Love you guys."

Mom and dad also arrived, and they all went to settle in to have some sleep. It was a tiring day.

The following morning, Jacques and Catherine were ready with their bags. The coffee was brewing in the kitchen. Gene was busy preparing snacks.

"Mom, so it's time to love and leave you, but don't worry, I promise I will see you every month and stay for a while." he attested.

"Yes, Jacques. Your father is not the man he used to be. His health is critical. Please do your best." mom pleaded.

"I know I can depend on you, my son. It's been a little tough at the company lately. So, be safe and we'll see you real soon." his dad told him.

"Yes, father. All will be fine, you'll see." Jacques confirmed.

"Uncle Franc, Aunty Gene, I would like to thank you, from my heart, for your hospitality and the great time I have spent in your beautiful home. You are the most loving family I've seen in a long time. I will personally make sure that Jacques visits regularly. I promise."

"Thank you, my dear. It was a pleasure to have you here." they both replied.

"You can drop us off at the drop-off, dad."

They stopped. Jacques took out their luggage. They kissed and hugged.

"Au revoir."

"We love you!" they shouted.

"Let me give Micah a call."

Jacques: Hey, Micah. How are things?

Micah: Hi! Good, good. How you?

Jacques: We are fine. We'll be landing around eleven am. See you at the airport. Ciao!

Micah: No problem, be safe. Bye!

"We finally alone, my love." Jacques smiled at her.

She got up and threw her arms around him. She kissed him left and right and left again on the cheeks, the forehead, and the nose. She hugged him tightly.

"I love you. Thank you for everything. It's back to reality. I've had the best holiday, ever." she added.

"Mm, sighed Jacques. I'm going into surgery a little later. I've some paper works to complete. What about you?"

"Oh, I will unwind and prepare for the year ahead. I can't wait to see the girls. I'm looking forward. Did I mention to you about the Milan Fashion Week? That is scheduled for February. The runway show is for one week. All the designers are from different places. It's an annual event. September and February. Beside the catwalk schedule, the show features a packed roster of events and parties, ending with the announcement of the prize winner on the last night." she added.

"No, you didn't mention it." he moaned.

The final boarding announcement was heard from where

they were sitting. They moved towards the boarding side. In the aircraft, Catherine sat by the window seat. As the plane rotated, before reaching the air, Catherine looked down at the city.

"Goodbye, Paris! Until next time." she smiled.

Jacques didn't have much sleep, so he had forty winks, on the flight. Catherine couldn't get Savannah out of her mind. She loathed that woman.

"How could she have a heart and be so cruel towards a real gentleman, of a husband? She thought by herself. I have to tell Jacques about this, or maybe I shouldn't. A real fool. They say there's a fool born every minute. That's what she is." she concluded her thoughts.

Jacques had a nice rest. The touchdown woke him.

"Hi, stranger. Have you slept well?" she asked sarcastically.

He smiled, with eyes almost still closed, stretching.

Micah was waiting on them at the arrival side.

"Hi guys," he said excitedly.

"Ah, how nice to see you, Micah! Wow! Did you polish her? She's looking so shimmering and shiny." he said surprisingly of his black BMW.

"Yeah, no worries. I enjoyed it, with pleasure."

They loaded the bags in the boot of the car and first dropped off Catherine.

"Thank you, Micah. Bye Jacques. I'll call you later."

Home sweet home, she thought out loud. A few hours later, she checked her post. She found a summons to appear in court. The family of Harold Evans filed a lawsuit against her and sued her for the value of the inheritance. They sued her for inheritance theft. She needed to appear in court within ten days.

"Oh no. Are they serious? I can't deal with this now, dammit!" she said angrily.

She shoved the papers in the drawer. She would not even page through it. Her face said, let battle commence.

She tidied up the apartment. Then ran herself a bath.

When she woke up the next morning, after the first sip of coffee, she forced herself to do one hundred sit-ups until her muscles cried. She took a cold and hot shower. Dressed smartly, did her hair and make-up. Her body was yearning for Jacques's embrace. Catherine experienced two opposite valence emotions. She was looking forward to seeing everyone at work, now this dark cloud is hanging over her. So much to deal with. She can't let the girls see her in this despondent state. She reframed her thoughts.

"I'm a strong resilient woman. I will adapt well in the face of adversity. Chin up, Catherine." she told herself.

She got to her boutique early. All the staff arrived together.

"Hey everybody. How nice to see all of you in one, piece. How were the holidays? Hope you enjoyed all the festivities."

"Hi, we are all well rested and ready for the new year!!"

"Wow, look at you! You look great, Catherine. We trust you had a wonderful time." Victoria and the others enquired.

"Thank you, yes, of course. He met my family, and they adored him. I met his family. They are all so sweet, except for Savannah, his brother's wife. That woman is a real she-devil and she is shrewd. But everything was lovely. So, welcome back to work, everyone. I missed you all." she said.

"Let's jump right into our first, minutes meeting and schedule for the new year ahead."

They all moved to the boardroom.

"As you all know about the Milan Fashion Week which is taking place in the last week of February. Victoria, as our store manageress, handles everything. Gary and Albert managing the men's side. One of the girls will have to go with me to Italy, whoever is available to go. Either Emily or Amelia. You girls have to decide. We will participate in the contest with our designs of last year, as well. We will be getting three new designer's lines of clothing in soon. We are the style educators. Many consumers don't have the time or the know-how to style themselves. Fashion is volatile and they are scared to try a new trend until boutiques show them. They walk in our store and they should be inspired and feel good about themselves in our clothes. We aim to inspire our customers, so when they buy our merchandise, they buy the experience."

"Definitely." the staff agreed.

"They buy memories and that is the equivalent to our business. We should cohesively communicate with our clients. We build an online community. Boutiques connect like-minded customers over a mutual interest in fashion, using live videos. Advertising, like we had with Facebook notifications and Instagram updates, and regular texts. Customers have a personal connection with the employees. You are the face of our brands."

"Yeah!!"

"Permit them to be your ambassadors. Appreciate them, because they have the power to make or break our brand. Customers like to discover new unique brands. We take risks, even should we fail. A trend might be popular in another country, but it could take time to reach popularity in our country. This is how we take risks. Learn what your customers want and we can't go wrong. Entrepreneurship isn't easy. As a team, we share strategies. Always invest in new marketing plans for our business. Our industry is growing and we succeed because we bring our unique personality and style to our customers. Our business is built with a heart. I could not have achieved this without my team. And I thank you all for the past year of success. Anyone has questions or would like to add anything?"

"We all good, this year we'll tackle the fashion world by storm, we'll grow bigger and better," they promised.

"Awe, thank you, guys."

She goes through the list.

"It looks like we've run out of time, so I guess we've covered everything and we are done here."

They all agreed. As the boutique doors opened, the customers entered.

Catherine took a drive up to Jacques's dental surgery. She first stopped at the bakery to buy some cake decadence. Sweet fresh cream pastries. Assorted custard cakes. Chiffon caramel covered with Cadbury ganache. Seems, she wanted to surprise him.

When she arrived, she went to the reception desk and asked the lady if she could see the doctor.

"Good morning, do you have an appointment?" the receptionist asked.

"No, I'm his friend. I wanted to bring him something sweet," she replied.

"Oh, okay."

The receptionist explained to Catherine that the doctor was busy with a patient and that he wouldn't be too long still.

His next appointment would be in an hour.

"I'll have a seat in the foyer and wait for the doctor," she said shyly.

CHAPTER 5

As the patient walked to the desk to make his follow-up appointment, Jacques came out to see if there was another patient.

"Next patient in an hour." the receptionist confirmed.

"Hey, what a nice surprise. Good to see you." he kissed her on the forehead in the foyer. He walked her into the surgery.

"What is all this yumminess, are we having a party?" he asked.

"Let's get us some coffee. He beeped for two coffees. You look a little tense, are you, all right?" he asked, concernedly.

"Yes, I'm good. I missed you."

She wrapped her arms around his waist and kissed him passionately. He held her so tight that, she couldn't breathe.

"I missed you too, my love. Can just hold you like this and never let you go. I do see you tonight, right?"

"Oh yes, of course. Unless you have another girlfriend lurking around?" she questioned.

"No way, I only have eyes for you, babe."

"So, this is where you work. Why have you decided to go into the dentistry field, instead of joining your father's empire? If you don't mind my asking." she added.

"Well, as a kid, I have been fascinated with healthy teeth. My parents wanted me to study medicine. That was on my cards, but then I opted to become a dentist. My love for caring for patients requires the ability to communicate and connect with people. What inspired me was to educate patients about, how to improve their oral health and boost their self-confidence. So, it's a rewarding career you can always feel good about. Due to the rise of our aging population, we'll require more dental treatments in the future. For me to eliminate their pain and put a dazzling smile on people's faces, makes me feel satisfied and very overjoyed." he explained to her.

"We give free services to the elderly people. And, also, it's a lucrative career path, as a dentist, my services will always be in demand."

"That is super awesome," she said.

"Did you plan to be a fashionista?"

While sitting on the sofa next to him, she lay her head on his lap.

"At first my dream was to be an air hostess. I wanted to travel the world. Then my parents advised me, that I would not be able to get married and have a family. That wouldn't have worked for someone like me. I decided to work hard enough, and still travel the world. There was modeling on the cards, but I always felt that I'm an ugly duckling and that I'm fat."

"Oh, my goodness, you look like a goddess." he interrupted.

"Then I said to my parents, Rebecca can be the model. I

opted for the fashion world. I studied fashion trends, sketched designs, and selected materials. I designed my merchandise, and sell them to ready-to-wear fashion stylists. I produced my brand fashion line. Working in the couture industry for four years. I met Harold at a function of my father's business associates. We fell in love and got married, one year later. I was at the peak of my career and we postponed, starting a family. It was God's plan for us. He knew better. If we did not delay having a child, I would have had a child growing up without a father." she said sadly.

He played with her hair, sliding his fingers through it. Parting her hair out of her face. He kissed her.

"Don't feel sad, you have me," he said caringly.

"Which brought me to where I am today. One month after Harold passed away, I opened up my boutique, dedicated to him," she said with tears in her eyes.

She felt emotional and tears streamed down her face. He held her tightly against his chest, as she sobbed.

"Don't worry, everything will work out for the best." he soothed her.

She finished her coffee.

"I will be fine, don't mind me, it's just one of my bouts of sadness. Jacques, I need to discuss something with you tonight."

"Sure, anytime."

She pulled herself together. Kissed him goodbye. He walked out of the surgery with her. He hugged her and she nodded at the receptionist.

"Good job, doctor, your next appointment will be here in ten minutes." she smiled.

"Jacques smiled from ear to ear."

Back at the boutique, Catherine needed to create some new designs for a theme of a new collection, fresh and original. Forecasting, what will be popular with consumers, she had to work on her brief towards specifications relating to color, fabric, and all the designs. She worked in PowerPoint for a while. Then she needed to take her developed patterns, and sample garments to the machinists preparing the final product. She needed to oversee production and negotiate with the suppliers. Two of her girls are her models, who try on the different outfits from a new collection to be presented. Vicky is her strong arm. She manages the marketing, finances, and all the other activities. Gary and Albert are in charge of the men's side. By late afternoon, the store was still very busy with customers.

"I had a long day. I'll be heading home, girls. She looked at them, thoughtfully. I know I can depend on all of you and leave everything in your capable hands. Promise me whatever happens, you will always have my back." she said with a crack in her voice.

"Of course, that is something you never have to fret about. You take it easy. We are all here for you." they all assured her.

She greeted and waved goodbye. On her way home, all she could think of was how to deal with the lawsuit. She didn't even touch those papers and read what they said. She couldn't understand why.

Why would they take her to court after all this time? Harold's family was never fond of her, but how could they stoop so low.

She first took a long, hot shower. Prepared something for supper. In case Jacques comes around early. She thought she'd make a French onion soup with croissants, Marquette, and salads. She took the summons with heavy hands. She read through the papers in disgust. They sued her for inheritance theft. What was stolen? She couldn't believe her eyes. Harold was a marine biologist. As working as a seafarer, his work was a great risk. He had a will, which his family found recently. After his funeral, Catherine never had any contact with any of them.

Catherine didn't expect Jacques too early, but he called to say that he was on his way. While on the phone, she called her mom.

Mom: Hi baby girl, how are you? You've been quiet lately, is everything ok?

Catherine: Hi Moms, yes, all good. Just been busy sorting out work stuff at the boutique. Planning the new year. How is everyone? I miss you guys.

Mom: They are all good, stay busy. You sound a little weary, my girl.

Catherine: I'm just a little tired and overworked. I'll be fine. Having an early night tonight.

Mom: All right my dear. You rest well. Take care of yourself. Love you lots. Bye.

Catherine: I will. Love you too, Mom. Bye, bye.

Jacques was at the door.

"Hey, this was earlier than I expected." they hugged.

"Hi, my love. Mm, what smells so good? The whiff makes my mouth water. Have you cooked for me?"

"No, it's only something light. I tried a new French recipe. At least I'm trying to."

"Wow, that looks great, let's dig in. I'm starving."

The table is set romantically, with candles as well. Soft music played in the background.

"This is delicious. You spoiling me. What was it you needed to talk to me about? It sounded crucial."

"Yes, later, that can wait." she smiled.

After supper, they sat on the puffy, two-seater sofa, with tall glasses of passion fruit mixed with soda. The chairs were reclined.

"It was a busy day at the surgery. I've seen eighteen patients today. The two, elderly ladies, when they left were so grateful to me and smiled happily and they said a prayer for me. That in return makes me so happy."

Tried as he might, Jacques could no longer concentrate on anything else, but her. He pulled her in his arms. Smothered her in a long, lingering kiss. Her heartbeat raced and her libido started revving up. A flare of heat erupted between them. It was only the two of them on the soft sofa. She twisted her body to his side. Straddle on top of him, onto his lap. She was able to kiss him more fully. Her breasts were smiling as her nipples showed through her top. As she was crouching on him, his hands ran down her back floating just over her ass. She was burning with desire. Her knees were on either side of him. They both could not deny that something slipped free of their souls and began to fill their hearts as their kiss deepened. Disposing of their clothes was easy. She unbuttoned his shirt, her fingers brushed against his chest, and the hunger rose between them both. She circled her moist tongue around his nipples, sweeping feather kisses around his neck, all over his chest. His cock was hard, as she unzipped his pants and ease the thick hard flesh. Moving her tongue from his balls right up to the shaft of his cock. Slipping it in her mouth, her lips watery, stroking him up and down with her hand, with each lick of her tongue. Pleasure sizzled over his nerve endings. It was more than heat, more like a blazing fire raging. He lifted her onto the back of the seat. He pressed her thighs apart. She wore a ribbed mini skirt, which rolled up to her hips. He pulled down her panty. He asked her to play with herself. She pumped her finger slowly, inside her vagina, and pulled free. The juices were glistening as he parted his lips to lick every fold of her pussy. He was dying for her. His hard body, tensed, and he could feel the need intensifying within him. Her moans and groans made him more desperate for the taste of her and the need to have her. His hands reached the rounded edge of her breasts. His tongue tacked into the folds of her flesh, driving her pussy closer to his lips. She needed him deep inside of her. She was burning with desire. He pressed her thighs further apart and pressed his cock inside of her. They stared into each other's eyes in dazed ecstasy as he began to move harder and faster strokes pumping inside of her. Her clit felt like a hard knot. He flipped her over on the seat, on top of him. He watched as the tight flesh of her pussy eased over his cock, sucking it into her body, with slow movements. He held on to her hips as she shifted and rolled them, slowly. He groaned as she slid down, thrusting him, taking his full length.

"Ride my dick, baby. Slide it up that tight, little pussy."

As he watched her orgasm, he felt his release exploding outside of her. Sensations ruptured through their bodies. She laid her head on his chest. He wrapped his arms around her. She felt safe in his arms.

"I love you."

"I love you too. Are you, hungry? I am." she said.

"Yeah, especially after you help us build a hell of an appetite. I'll just take a quick, shower, I will be there now."

They went into the kitchen and ate the leftovers. After he finished his Marquette and coffee. He asked her what is on her mind. She looked at him and began explaining to him the summons.

"When we arrived home, the other day I was served with a summons. I found it in my post. My husband's family filed a lawsuit against me. They sued me for inheritance theft." she whined.

"Oh, my goodness gracious me. How can that even be possible?" he asked angrily.

"The family recently came across a will of Harold, but that was before we got married. He was a seafarer. Working in the maritime industry, was a risky job. The employees needed to have a legal, valid will in place. Harold wasn't quiet, close to his family. They treated him with disrespect. They never approved of anything he did, it was more like he was an outsider. Especially, when he chose to marry me."

"He was a good husband, he cared for me and loved me dearly." she cried.

"He had a new, last will, drawn up after we got married. He had two separate life insurance policies. We lived in our own home. One of his colleagues at work, whom he was very close to and could trust, was appointed as the executor of his estate. I was named as the sole beneficiary of his estate. Three weeks after his funeral, I was contacted by his place of work. They set up a meeting and I had to attend. The knowing Jacques is in her room. She followed her plans to watch movies. She felt at ease, knowing in the back of her mind, that the court case can't get out of hand, as she has legal documents to prove.

Time flew, and after two movies, it was around five am in the morning. She went into the room. Jacques was still in never-never land.

She decided to take the day off. As she laid quietly next to him. His eyes opened slightly. She glimpsed at him. She slips her fingers through his dark, black hair, and felt deep affection. The warmth, the intimacy, the special connection. She could feel it in her whole being. Cuddling up behind him. He turned around and looked into her eyes.

"Wow, what a beautiful sight to wake up to. I could do this every morning." he kissed her gently.

"I hope you had a good night's rest. Would you like some coffee?" she kissed him back.

"Sure, in a minute."

He wrapped his arms around her.

The smell of her perfume, her luscious hair, he just gets turned on instantly. She could feel perspiration dampening her hair. He held her so tight, that she could hardly breathe.

"Let me just hold you in my arms for a while. Catherine, please promise me that you will never let anything come between us. I love you more and more each day. You make my soul move." he confessed.

"My dearest love, you may be one person to the whole world, but to me, you are the whole world. There's no other love, like our love." she smiled.

He kissed her on her forehead.

breath and had chest pains. He is already anemic, which makes him feel tired and weak.

"You have to take it easy, Franc. What is troubling you, my dear?" Gene asked worriedly.

"Is everything good at work?"

"Some things do not add up at work in the finances. I've checked inventory levels for the unexplained decline. The company's inventory levels do not reflect the company's revenue. This is an indication that embezzlement is present in the company."

Franc found this increasingly puzzling. Gene was in shock. She slid her reading glasses onto the eyes that were on her head. She took a look at some of the paper works Franc browsed through.

"Maybe there could be errors in the system or some blunders?" she suggested.

"This demise could not come at a better time. When you are unwell or is this the problem that causes you to feel ill?" she wanted to know.

At that moment, they heard Arthur and Juliette arriving. They made it a priority to pop around there every day to check on mom and dad.

Juliette brought them hot supper. She does so almost every night and would arrange with Gene, not to cook. Zoe kissed her Pepe and meme and went straight to the play area outside. She set the table in the dining room area. Arthur sat down with his mom and dad. Angel was busy in her room, sitting with her legs over, up on the sofa, her laptop on her thighs. Juliette warmed up the pie Gene prepared earlier that day, as well.

Juliette called out to all of them that dinner is being served.

"Bonjour, how's everyone?" Angel ran to the play park to get Zoe.

"Hullo, how's my little pumpkin." Zoe jumped on Angel and she swung her around in circles.

"Let's go eat, babes."

At the table, the atmosphere seems rather somber.

"Yummy, our favorite Zoe, Chicken a La King." Angel tried to cheer them up.

"Are you feeling better, dad?" Arthur asked.

"Yeah, I guess. I need to rest. I've been looking at the financial reports, and there is an indication of massive embezzlement going on in the company. That can only happen in the accounts department."

"Oh. That is atrocious. We'll have to get to the bottom of this." Arthur insisted.

"Dad, I'm sorry to interrupt. I think you should stay at home for a few weeks. Arthur and Pierre are capable of handling the situation. They will sort it out." Angel demanded.

"Angel is right. You need to take it easy. Don't worry about the company issues. You can depend on your sons." mom added.

"I agree 100%," Juliette said.

"I spoke to Catherine earlier on the phone. I meant to tell you, mom. I'm going to spend some time at Jacques, in the next week. Catherine invited me to stay at her place. She also asked me to assist her with some legal matters. Would that be okay, dad?" she asked.

"I suppose that is fine, if your mother is all good with it," dad approved.

"Yes, Juliette is always around. She's my other daughter. You go and enjoy your stay at your brother."

The tea tray was on the table, when dad poured tea from the heavy teapot, with a frail, shaking hand. Arthur glanced at him. He is the Chief Executive Officer. He is responsible for managing his father's company's overall operations. His father depends on him, how is it possible, that he could not pick up any discrepancies. What about Pierre, he is managing and oversees the daily implementation of the financial department of the company. Why did they not detect, anything wrong? They need to resolve this. He feels, disgruntled. Like they're failing their father.

Angel was busy clearing up the table.

"Juliette, I hear Zoe is attending Kinder Garten. Does she like it?" Angel, asked.

"She loves to interact with the children and connect easily. I hope it stays that way, as she doesn't like separation."

"Oh, you're a star!" she kissed Zoe on her head.

A while later, Arthur and Juliette had to go home. Mom and dad settled in. Angel opened her laptop as she left it, before dinner time. She's busy researching advocacy.

Early the following morning, mom's standing by the kitchen bench, swigging down her morning coffee. Angel went to the pantry, took out a box of cornflakes, and pour some straight into her mouth.

"Angel!" mom yells.

"Use a bowl."

Her mouth was full, she shook her head and point to her watch. She waved to mom and headed to the front door. Mom rushed after her.

"Wait, where are you rushing to this morning?" she called out.

"I'm going shopping to go to Jacques. I'm going sooner. See you later mom, au revoir!" she said.

She spent almost half a day shopping at Galleries-Lafayette Hausman. She bought all kinds of gifts for Catherine and Jacques. Angel is very excited to go to London.

One week later, Franc rested at home. He needed to focus on getting better. He and Gene took long walks, every day to keep fit and do light exercises. What he needs now is to eliminate distractions, but this is very hard at this stage. He couldn't rest his mind, knowing something was very wrong.

"Gene, I think I'm going in later this afternoon."

"Are you sure, love? Is it not too soon?"

"No, I'm good, I've rested well. Don't worry about me," he confirmed.

Franc could not rest. His anxiety got the better of him. On his way to the office, he took his usual route, past the school where Lois and Jules attend. He spotted Savannah talking to a man. She got into the guy's car. Franc thought he will pull over and watch her. Half an hour passed and they were still in the car. It was time for the school to dismiss. She got out of the car and from her body language, any fool could see, that something is cooking. They kissed. Franc knew his son had a troubled marriage. He did not expect this, though. He couldn't make out who the guy was. He reached his office to do some more digging.

Arthur and Pierre were busy in meetings the whole day. They were busy with new lines of perfume. This is the most intriguing part of the manufacturing of perfumes. Oils are extracted from plant substances, by steam distillation and expressed. The oils are then dissolved in the alcohol to rise. Heat is used to evaporate the alcohol, which leaves a higher concentrated oil on the bottom. This particular process is crucial. It needs the perfect ratio of alcohol to scent, that determines whether the parfum is, Eau de toilette or Eau de parfum. Oil-based, water-based. Fine perfume is often aged for months or years after it is blended. Each essential oil and parfum have three notes. Top notes, central notes, and the base notes. Anything other than the perfect process of developing the perfume will be a big blunder and lost cost to the company. Arthur and Pierre are very professional in their jobs. He wouldn't want to worry their minds with all these spectacles that would unfold, soon. Again, he came across more fraudulent activities. He had no substantial authentication. This would be an assignment for auditors, but in the back of his mind, he does have a suspect.

He drove back home in utter revulsion. He decided to keep everything classified for now, until he can substantiate the allegations.

Back in London, the boutique was bustling as usual. Catherine was busy having a meeting with suppliers. She's doing branding and networking. Marketing the new apparel fashion label, for the blogger focused on online marketing strategies. Vicky created a new website with a new logo and mission statement and Catherine loaded all the new images of the fashion line. They installed a new big-screen television on the men's side, for advertising, as well.

She was just thinking of Angel when she called.

Catherine: Hey, was just thinking of you.

Angel: Hi, I've been busy getting my priorities in order. How's Jacques?

Catherine: He's been busy at the practice. I haven't seen him in a couple of days. He's busy helping his friend, Micah move house. He calls regularly. I mentioned to him you coming to stay with me.

Angel: All right, great! As I wanted to let you, I will be on my way by Friday. If that is okay with you?

Catherine: Oh, wow. That would be amazing. Let's surprise Jacques. He knows that you coming, but has no clue when. I'll book you a one-way ticket, so you can decide when to return. I'll pick you up at the airport.

Angel: Awesome. Thank you, merci. I see you soon, I can't wait. Ciao, ciao!

Catherine: Bye!

CHAPTER 6

Mom and dad were sitting on the sofa in the living room, watching a movie. Angel went into the kitchen. She made three cups of Chocolate Chaud for them. On the tray, she had a bowl of assorted mixed nuts and biscuits.

"Merci, Cherie. You were busy today."

"Yes, mom. Friday morning, I'm leaving for London. Could you please drop me at the airport, dad? I need fifty boxes of parfum to market at Catherine's boutique. What do you think, dad?"

"That is not a bad proposal, hey! Have you spoken to her about this?"

"Not yet, but we'll talk about it when I get there."

Mom stared at her. "You quiet, brilliant, my child." mom said proudly.

"If you like, we can add some cosmetic products, too."

"No, let's start with the Eau de perfume for ladies and gents.

"I'll get you a box with twenty-five ladies and twenty-five men's pure perfume."

"Are you going to be all right, dad? I don't like leaving you two all alone. As I'm not sure when I will be returning. Could be two weeks or longer. I'm going with her to the fashion show in Milan as well."

"Oh, that's great. We'll be fine. Arthur and Pierre are around. Juliette is also like my own daughter." mom and dad assured.

They enjoyed the movie and togetherness and went to settle in. Late Friday afternoon, Angel loaded her luggage in her father's car. They drove her to the airport.

"You have a lot of luggage. Seems you leaving for a whole year." laughed dad.

"Oh, you know women, dad. Je Vous Aime Maman et papa." she greeted and kissed them on either side of the face.

"You be safe ma fille!"

Catherine called Jacques to inform him that she won't be seeing him in the evening, as she had to go to her mom's place. She first wanted Angel to settle in, then surprise Jacques. He was still busy helping Micah. She drove to the airport to pick up Angel. She would arrive in a few minutes.

"Bonjour, Catherine, so good to see you!"

"Hey, I'm so excited. We going to have a good time. We'll first settle you in at home. I'll take you to dinner tonight."

"Yeah, I'm starving!"

"What would you like to eat?"

"You know what I eat everything. You choose, I'm not fussy." she nodded.

They pulled into her driveway. Angel was very impressed with Catherine's beautiful place.

"Wow, just elegant. I could stay here forever. I love your apartment." she laughed.

They carried her suitcases to her room. After she showed Angel the rest of the place, they took a drive out into the city, searching for a good restaurant.

"Ah, I know, we'll go to, Cigalon. They have the finest food on the menu. You'll love it."

"You look so good, Catherine. Do you always dress up elegantly?"

"Thanks, well I have to. I have to be the face of the boutique."

"I love your style, it's gorgeous. In my bags, I brought you, different kinds of pure perfume for your couture line of designer fashion that will work well with perfume. I asked my father for just a few samples. He gave me fifty for ladies and gents, from the finest ones, packaged in wrapped boxes. He thought it was a brilliant idea."

"That is fantastic. We plan to combine brand, viral and digital into one comprehensive strategic marketing plan. Vicky, my right hand at work is busy running a campaign ad to create brand awareness. That is just a wonderful scheme. We can make short video adverts with you and the perfume. Would you like to be one of my models, too?"

"Oh wow! That would be great!"

"Two of my girls at work are my cast models, to bring my collection to life. But you could also add some flair and flavor to my runway shows. You will stand out. French girl in London."

"Perfecto! Ooh-la-la, I can't wait. Let's eat!"

They arrived at the restaurant. The waiter was friendly and polite, and gave them a nice cozy spot, overlooking London Bridge. It was a cold night, Angel wore her jacket, which Catherine bought her.

"Oh, this is spectacular. I might even extend my stay."

They ordered different kinds of foods. Grilled beef onglet, Lamb breast, salads with hot caramelized wings, and Crème Brule for desserts. Also, a hot pot of English tea.

"We'll surprise Jacques tomorrow. What about you, are you seeing anyone special?"

"No, I had a cute guy, Mathieu, but I shook him off quick. He wanted to have an open relationship and see other girls as well. What is special about that? That wasn't my forte."

"That's the spirit." Catherine nodded.

"Paris is called the City of Love and romance. I haven't found the right person, I suppose. But I like to be a free spirit, anyway."

"My sister, Rebecca, you'll meet her on Sunday, she goes out with her friends, but have no special boyfriend. I have lunch with my family on Sundays. It's like a tradition with my mother."

"Oh, lovely!"

As the waiter served their food, he noticed a French accent coming from Angel.

"Bon appetite!" he said.

"Merci beaucoup!" Angel replied.

"Ooh, yummy. I'm going to have a feast. I haven't eaten all day. So tomorrow we have to go over your documents for the court case." Angel said.

They were dining for hours and still ordered more desserts. Dark chocolate Moelleux with yogurt sorbet and peach lemon verbena sorbet with almond tuille. It was late when they got home. They took a shower and off to bed. They would have a busy day ahead.

Catherine left early the Saturday morning. She didn't want to wake Angel. She left a note in the kitchen for her.

'Hi, I didn't want to disturb you. Make yourself at home. Go through the documents. See you later...Love Catherine.'

By late afternoon, Angel woke up and stretched. She slept like a log. She read the note on the kitchen table and poured some Coco-Pops into a bowl. She had coffee and sat on the sofa. Turned on the television, and watch some London news.

"This is a posh apartment." she thought to herself.

She walked around and saw this beautiful, gold-rimmed frame on the wall of one of the rooms. It was dedicated to Harold Evans. They were a beautiful couple. The words said it all.

She sat at the dining room table, to analyze the court papers. She drew up a list of the proceedings. Catherine called her.

Catherine: Hi, sleepy head. You, okay?

Angel: Bonjour, yes, I'm good. Just had some breakfast in the afternoon. I guess in London I can do things differently. Where's Jacques?

Catherine: He's busy at the surgery. He'll probably come around later. I'll be back home in the next hour.

Angel: All right. I finished the list of proceedings for the court hearing. We'll go through it. I'm going to grab a shower and see you later. Ciao, ciao.

Catherine: Bye!

Jacques dropped by at the boutique. Catherine was busy in her office finishing up.

"Hey, stranger." she smiled from ear to ear.

"God, I missed you." he kissed her and hold her tight.

"What have you been up to? I haven't seen you all week. Let's go. I see you at my place."

MASQUED LOVE *BOOK 1*

"What are the plans for tonight, are we going somewhere, romantic or staying in?" he asked before getting into his car.

She stood by his window leaning forward, towards him.

"I'm not sure hey, we have to decide later."

As they pulled up into the driveway, Angel was standing behind the door when they both entered.

"Surprise!" she shouted excitedly.

Jacques's jaws dropped and his eyes stared in disbelief.

"C est, genial. This is a surprise." they grabbed each other and kissed.

"I didn't expect you so soon, maybe closer to the court date, but I'm happy that you're here. How's everyone?"

"Well, father is doing much better now. Mom insisted he took off from work. He has since been at home for the past two weeks. He went back yesterday for a short while."

"Yeah, I called him yesterday. He sounded distressed. How are things at the office? I promised them to come soon."

"There seems to be something fishy going on in the company. Dad has been researching the company's financials. According to him, some things, are not adding up. I hope this is not the reason for dad being ill at ease." she exclaimed.

"That is strange, he never mentioned anything to me. I'll have a word with Arthur and Pierre."

"I suppose he doesn't want to worry you. It's very hard on him, you not being there. He knows you are very busy at the surgery. He might have a premonition about something. This is why he's been acting weird and apprehensive, lately. He doesn't want to discuss these things over the phone, maybe he planned to tell you when you go home."

"Speaking of dad. I mentioned to him about marketing the parfum here in London at Catherine's boutique. He thought it was a wonderful gesture. He gave me a box of fifty parfums. They're only samples, to see how it will work. Isn't that great, Jacques?" she smiled.

"And I got you both some gifts," she added.

"That's awesome. Thank you for the gifts."

"All right. What's for dinner? Shall we go out?" Catherine asked.

"I'd love to," Angel replied.

"Excusez Moi, why are you staying here and not at my place? Aren't you the one who says nobody should ever invade anyone else's space?" Jacques said disapprovingly.

"Well, never you mind. Catherine invited me to stay with her. It's so much more fun here with her. I love it here. We going to paint this magical town, red. Speaking of red. It's almost Valentines, day soon. Even though I don't have a date." she laughed.

"You two are too amusing." Catherine laughed out loud.

"Anyone up for pizza? I'm so hungry, I can eat a horse." Angel said.

Jacques raised his brows, surprised, yet cynical as realization dawned. Given the favor of his formidable sister, Angel would not need his support in establishing her social position.

"That would be delicious." Catherine's eyes widened, but she laughed.

She glided her arm around Jacques.

"Let's go dine. Jacques will drive us to the best Piazza restaurant in town."

"London is breathtaking, with all its architecture and also the lively nightlife. No doubt, I can get used to this life in time." Angel murmured.

The bright lights of Piccadilly swung into view. Half an hour later, while driving through the streets of London, they pulled up outside at the restaurant in Berkley Square. Capturing her wide gaze, he smiled lovingly at Catherine.

"Is this how my next couple of weeks going to be?" he whispered in her ear.

Catherine smiled.

They went upstairs and waited to be seated at a cool spot. They ordered different kinds of pizza on the menu. Angel glared at Jacques, but his eyes were fixed on Catherine.

"Jacques, I suggest you speak to your brother. Pierre, seems very withdrawn lately. He visits us alone these days. That normally happens, when he has major outbursts with Savannah. She's a real pain in the neck. She keeps the boys away, as well. Appalled, by the fact that she could overlook her apparent insensitivity. She would do what she deemed right, regardless of any harm she causes her boys and husband. That woman is promiscuous." Angel complained.

"Yes, I'll go there, when Catherine goes to Italy. I might stay for the week. Other than that, we shall probably go cycling on the weekends."

"We'll only be away one weekend, duh," Angel said sarcastically.

It was Saturday, evening, the place was packed. After twenty minutes, the waiter put the piping hot pizzas on the table. The aroma was to die for.

"Mm, yumminess." Angel licked her lips.

"Enjoy." said the waiter.

"This is the best pizza I've ever had."

She never enjoyed anything so much before.

"Tomorrow, we have the usual Sunday at my parents. Jacques do you have any plans?" she asked.

"Yeah, still busy at Micah's place. We going to be quite a while still. You two can go and enjoy yourselves." he replied.

"Micah, whose Micah? When do I get to meet him?" Angel asked.

"He is my friend. We belong to the same cycling club, Penge. We regularly cycle through Royal Parks and along the Thames River. We've been friends for a long time now since I moved to London. You'll meet him soon. Don't worry, I'll hook you up." Jacques said.

"You're a star, Jacques," Angel said.

"Why do you say that?"

"Just because!"

"Don't be disappointed, if it doesn't work. I'll give it my very best shot for you both. The hooking up with your friend." she said.

Angel looked lonely. After they finished their pizza, they went for a walk.

As they strolled down the streets hand-in-hand, they looked like any other couple in love. The Mayfair walk took them through the side streets of London and the secret gardens.

The fresh bite of the nippy air was about to cross in their direction. They headed back to the car.

"This was a wonderful evening, merci, merci to both of you," Angel said.

Pulling her hood over her head from the chills.

"It's a pleasure." they both replied.

"You must take Angel to the King Cross Mall, which is London's shopping gem. She loves shopping. She will find everything, there, she can't find in France." he joked.

"You funny!" Angel chuckled.

Jacques squeezed her hand and kissed it. His hand rubbed between her thighs. She glanced at him smiling. While driving home, Angel was sitting in the back seat of his car, and she nodded off for a while.

"When are you going to Micah? Are staying over at my place? It's late." "I'm going to him tomorrow. If you want me to stay, I will."

As the garage door opened, Angel woke up.

"I need a bed, I'm exhausted." she went to settle in.

"Good night."

Jacques wrapped his arms around her and she nestled into the crook of his shoulder. He sighed, happily.

"This is rather nice, it seems as if the most difficult thing to do, is to find time alone with you," he complained and kissed her lips.

She walked into the kitchen and turned on the kettle.

"Ooh! Coffee, lovely."

He dimmed the lights down low in her bedroom. He flipped through her cd collection and chose Ivory Bell.

The soothing love songs float through the apartment. Picking up the remote, she turned it down a notch.

"Can't have it on too loud, we have a guest in the house."

"She sleeps like the dead, usually." he grinned.

She undressed to take a shower. Jacques was already stalk-naked in bed.

"Look at me, I'm in love." he sings with the music playing.

Warm approval shone in Catherine's big black eyes.

"I've been yearning for this moment. Oh, Catherine, you are so beautiful. You smell so good."

Holding her, kissing her gently on her neck. He rolled her over, caressing her rounded breasts. Feather kissed around her nipples. He thrust his middle finger down, and slide it gently over her folds. Caressing her with gentle touches. He found her clit, rubbing it in small circles. Desire was burning up inside of her. Slowly he moved down her thighs with his lips. He tasted her wetness. The smell of her, the sweet taste of her, so close against him, skin to skin.

"Oh, Jacques. Lick me. Take me. You drive me wild." she whined.

Arching, impatiently against his mouth. She grabbed his hair with both hands, as his tongue flickered her sweet spot and folds of her pussy. Her skin was hot and damp. Her pussy was wet and open ready for him. She tightened her legs around him, feeling the strands of his hair against her thighs, which was its own provocation.

He was tormented with desire. She grabbed his hard, erected cock, encircled it in her hand, and caressed it with gentle strokes. She took it in her mouth. She was desperate to have him inside of her. Her tongue licked around the top part in circular movements, then right down into her mouth. He made glorious sounds and delicious moans of pleasure. He flipped her over and drove his tongue again deep inside of her. So wet now, she could hear the slippery sound every time he drove back into her. He entered her with a smooth, hard thrust.

"I want to own you. You're mine, body, and soul," he whispered.

In his ear, she whispered.

"Hard please."

"That's it, that's it, my darling!" he said.

His thrust gained a steady tempo, she licked his nipples, moving her hands down his abs, clamping her legs around his waist. Driving him deeper inside of her, until he explodes. He pulls out and squirts all over her body.

"Sensational, oh God, I love you," he said.

"Love you too," she said softly.

The next day, Jacques left in the early hours of Sunday morning. He kissed her and said he'll call her later. By mid-morning, before Catherine and Angel were on their way to her parent's house, she explained the step-by-step court proceedings to her.

"On the first court appearance, the court clerk will read out the offense to the defendant. What you have been charged with. You will be asked to plead guilty or not guilty. This is called the arraignment, as well as your legal and constitutional right." she explained.

"You should plead not guilty at the arraignment. The judge presiding, will set a date for trial. Pleading not guilty, leaves all your options open. A contest mention is a step that is used to resolve the matters before the matter is adjourned off to a contested hearing – a plea of not guilty. The purpose of a preliminary hearing would be for the judge to determine if there were sufficient evidence to bind you over to stand trial. In your circumstances, you are protected from criminal charges." she further advised.

"So, we are all set for next week. Thank you. I have a general idea of how it works. I just know, and I feel safe because you are there for me. You are outstanding, my dear." Catherine told her.

She opened up the suitcase and took out the gifts she bought Catherine in Paris. She handed her a box with a sentimental gift. In the cute box was a couple's heart, a Swarovski crystal necklace with a matching bracelet. She gave her a fur jacket, scarves, and a pretty bed throw. For Jacques, she bought Non-alcoholic bubbly and assorted chocolates. Amongst the personalized mugshot sets with 'I love you Catherine and I love you Jacques' imprinted on them.

"Aww, you're so sweet. Thank you, thank you!"

"You're welcome. I like you since the first time we have met. My brother isn't like most men. He loves deeper than anyone I've ever known. He doesn't just fall for anyone, so for him to love you as much as he does, must mean, you're amazing. You mean everything to him therefore you mean everything to me. You are special."

"You going to make me cry."

She wrapped her arms around Angel and hugged her tightly.

"You're a glitter bomb of glory. I am so happy and privileged to have you here," she said with a kind heart.

"Now we going to dress up elegantly for lunch at my mom's. Let me show off my boyfriend's gorgeous sister."

CHAPTER 7

On their way, Catherine was telling Angel that she was being sued for three million pounds.

"That was probably the value of the estate, at that time. He never had life insurance policies on that will. They are not aware he had a last will drawn up. But you know what Angel? I feel sorry for them. I pity them. When all this is over, I want to grant them the three million pounds. That would be for his parents, from him. What do you think, Angel?"

"Well, that's a lot of money, Catherine. But if that is what your heart desires, then you do just that. Go for it." she said with a smile.

She pulled into the driveway of her parents' massive house.

"Ooh, what a lovely place. You grew up here Catherine?"

"Yeah, this was home. Memories warm you up from the inside."

They both dressed very smartly in cocktail dresses, sporting fur jackets and high stiletto heels.

Catherine entered with a bang.

"Hi, everybody. I'd like to introduce to you all, Jacques's little sister, Angelique."

"Angelique, this is my father James Darcy and mother Jemima."

"Monsieur, Mademoiselle. It's great connecting with you."

"My sister, Rebecca."

"Thank you, a pleasure to meet you too." they all greeted and gave her a warm welcome.

"Gosh, look at you two. Gorgeous, like models." dad said.

"Speaking of models, Angelique brought me some of her father's perfume range along, so we will include them in our line of fashion. She will be my model as well." Catherine explained.

"That's lovely. How long are you staying, Angelique? Are you doing modeling?" mom Jemima asked.

"My stay is indefinite, aunty Jemima. Catherine invited me to go with her to the Milan show. Oh, no. Not in my wildest dreams. I just finished my J.D. degree in August of last year, so I am a lawyer by trade. I'm taking a break from all the studies, Madame."

"Well, you certainly have that supermodel looks."

"Merci, thank you," she said smiling.

"How do you like London?" James asked.

"Oh, it's beautiful and lively, but more laid back here. I love it here. I find it also more vibrant and exciting. People are very friendly." she replied.

"Could stay here forever." she laughed.

Half an hour later, they were all sitting in the lounge. The brothers with their wives arrived. They all meet and greet.

Abby, Bella, and Ethan squeezed and kissed everyone, and off they went to play outside.

The table was already set, so they all went to take their seats.

"Lunch is served." dad called.

On the table was a variety of delicious foods, roast meats, roast potatoes, and accompaniments. Yorkshire puddings, stuffing, gravy, salsa salads. Curries with rice.

The girls, Andrea, Olivia, and Sofia, each brought along different desserts.

"Seems like a lunch, fit for a King," Angel said.

"Could you please pass me the stuffing, Miles?" Catherine asked.

"Where's Jacques today?" Richard asked.

"He's busy helping a friend today. His moving house. We'll come again soon, Richard."

"Oh, all right."

"The foods are delicious, thank you, I feel honored to be a guest in your beautiful home. Thank you, everybody." Angel said.

Lunch went on for hours. Everyone had something to ask Angel. They all placed big orders for parfum with Angel. Everybody had great admiration for her. Rebecca thought she might go with her sister to the Milan show too if she will be available. Colin and Olivia said they would try to come to the Milan show as well if they could manage.

Catherine chose not to tell her parents about the lawsuit. She wouldn't want to trouble them over this. As she knows them, they will be sick with worry about a court case.

It was early evening, the ladies had English tea in the gardens. Playing some ball games with the little ones.

"You have to go now, my dear. We don't want you to be so late on the road."

"Yes, you right mom. We'll leave now."

"Au revoir, everybody. It was a pleasure to have met all you beautiful people. I'm hoping to invite all of you to meet Jacques's family one day. Thank you once again." Angel said.

"The pleasure is ours. Drive safe, girls."

"Will do, mom." Catherine kissed and embraced them all in tight hugs. "Love you all!" she shouted.

On their way home, Jacques called. They have him on speaker phone.

Jacques: Hi ladies, you are not home yet. How was lunch?

Catherine: Hi, we driving home as we speak. Lunch was wonderful.

Angel: Hi. Brother! What's happening? Lunch was fantastic. Lovely hosts.

Jacques: That's great. Yes, they are the best. Catherine, we are still very busy, so I won't see you guys in a couple of days.

Catherine: Oh, that is fine. We are extremely tired anyway. You keep well. We'll see you soon. Bye.

Jacques: Sure, love. Stay safe. Love you, bye!

The slow drive back home allowed Angel to look at the beautiful scenery. She made certain she snapped photos of the pristine scenery. Most picturesque views. When they reached their destination, they retreated to their rooms and went straight to bed.

Early Wednesday morning, Catherine had coffee on the kitchen bench, while Angel had cereal for breakfast, before getting ready. She wore black, slacks with a white blouse. Ready for a court hearing. She's frozen, momentarily paralyzed as she tried to process all this. She's not sure what to expect. Thoughts of, what if she gets locked up went through her mind. Angel wore her black knee, high dress, and black robe, and nodded to Catherine that she was ready. She assured her everything will work out fine.

"Catherine, you don't have to worry about this, I will have it under control." Angel tried to calm her nerves.

"Thank you, I know. It's just normal intense anxiety. I feel safe with you."

On their way to the Supreme Court, the drive seemed long. They entered the courtroom, which looked eerie. Catherine has never been in a place like this before. It was rather empty. She saw from her side, Mr. and Mrs. Evans and their attorney, Advocate Roberto. She greeted them and they turned their faces away. Everyone settled down.

The presiding Judge Quintin John Turner asked Catherine's lawyer if the defendant would like to have the charge read to her.

"No. Your honor, my client understands the charge."

"How does she plead for the charge of inheritance theft?"

"She's pleading not guilty, Your honor."

At the arraignment, Catherine was asked if she wanted to take care of the matter today. Angel was asked if she would like to speak to the prosecutor, to see if they can agree. The judge asked Angel to approach the bench. He mentioned to Angel that she may suggest a resolution, or set a trial date. She spoke to the prosecutor, who had legally admissible evidence, sufficient to prove the defendant's guilt beyond a reasonable doubt.

Angel showed her documentation of the last will of the late Mr. Harold Evans' estate dated after the documents Advocate

Roberto had. She did not have to have any closing arguments in the case.

It was already clear that the evidence the prosecutor had, was null and void. It clearly states that Catherine Darcy Evans was the sole beneficiary listed in the will of the late Mr. Harold Evans. They were both called to the judge's box for contest mention. The prosecutor explained to the judge the adverse claim in the court of the plaintiff. They would like to contest the probate of the will.

After cross-examination, Advocate Roberto was also present in the meeting. The judge read out the final verdict.

"All rise. It is stated that the evidence of inheritance theft, absolutely failed to prove the guilt of the accused beyond a reasonable doubt. Catherine Darcy Evans was acquitted on all counts. The case was dismissed."

"My life sucks." her face crumbling.

"Listen to me. The only people who know the truth about your feelings, are you and me." Angel said.

She laughs nervously and runs her fingers through her hair. She let out a slow breath and shook her head. Her eyes flash with excitement and feel terrible at the same time.

She sighed a sigh of relief and got up to embrace Angel with a big hug.

"Go after them and explained to them what's on your mind."

Mr. and Mrs. Evans vacated the courtroom. The look on their faces showed despair and bitterness.

Catherine met up with them outside. They felt let down and betrayed. She called them mom and dad. They refused to look at her, let alone talk to her. She got all emotional and stood right in front of them, with tears in her eyes.

"I know you feeling very deluded right now. I am very sorry for all this. I've not been unfaithful to you two, I swear by God."

"What do you want from us, Catherine? You have caused us enough anguish. Please leave us alone!" Mr. Evans said.

With tears streaming down her face, she explained to them, how much she loved and adored their son and that he'll forever be in her heart. She further explained to them about the life insurance policies he had and that she opened her boutique in dedication to him. She was sobbing very sadly now.

"I want to grant you the three million pounds in honor of your son. This was my intention, before the court hearing."

"Oh my! I can't believe what I'm hearing. Are you sure you could do this, Catherine?" they asked desperately.

After Angel wounded up her court case documentation and thanked the judge, she walked out and saw Catherine and the Evans in a beautiful bear hug embrace. Emotions were running high.

"Oh, my dear child, you have no idea what this means to us. We are struggling to make ends meet. I'm not too fit to work anymore. And our house is at risk. While going through our documents, we found Harold's will. This is how we concluded. We should have rather confronted you first. We are so sorry to drag you into this. Our apologies. Harold was a good son. He had his moments and was always distant, but he took care of us." Mr. Evans explained emotionally.

"Thank you, thank you. May God bless you abundantly." they prayed.

"You're welcome. I will come to you soon to do the transfer into your account, dad," she promised.

She kissed them on the cheeks and waved goodbye.

"Now this, calls for a celebration," Angel shouted. Smiling with an open mouth.

"Aww, thank you. I'm so proud of you Angel. I don't know what I would have done without you. You are a star. You are a ray of hope. I feel so much better. I feel good." she almost cried.

"It's a pleasure, my dear."

At the boutique, Jacques was already waiting on them. He tried to call them, but both their mobiles were switched off.

He stood outside having a smoke when he saw the two of them walking towards the boutique. They were smiling and looked high-spirited. By their expressions, he felt, alleviated. He was quite disturbed about the situation.

"Hey man, good to see you. The case was dismissed. Your sister sorted everything and the matter was resolved. It was better than I anticipated. Your sister is the best."

Angel pulled Jacques by the nose. "Advocate Angelique Dupont, at your service, Monsieur," and she gave him a bow.

They all laughed loudly, entering the boutique.

"Hi everybody, I'd like you to meet Jacques's sister, Angelique Dupont."

"Hullo, Angelique, a pleasure to meet you." they all shook hands.

"Hi, the pleasure is all mine. You have a pretty classy boutique here."

"Thank you."

"She will be joining us at the boutique for a short while. We going to introduce her father's range of perfumes in our store. And before I forget, she will also accompany me and

Emily to the Milan Fashion week in two weeks. She's an extrovert. You'll all love her."

Angel was now brimming with excitement.

"The fragrances can definitely work with your exclusive line of designs, Catherine."

"Yeah, for sure. Make yourself at home."

Jacques looked at his watch and said he had an afternoon appointment, and that he had to run.

"We are still very busy for the next few days. Talk to you later."

He kissed her like the French does, brushing the side of the cheeks. More like kissing air and he rushed off.

"Would you like to go to the movies tonight, Angel? We can first grab a bite to eat somewhere."

"Yeah, that would be interesting. I want to first browse around this beautiful place. Your charming staff also put an extra sparkle in your boutique."

"Thank you. Aww, you are so, kind. Yes, fine. No rush. I'll book the tickets online. You take your time."

"Catherine, I meant to tell you. That frame in the back room, commemorating your husband, is very significant. Very pretty."

"Yes, he was a good man, I loved him very much. And you know, I'm feeling satisfied that we've made peace. I feel so much better since the court hearing. Everything happens for a reason. Every effect has a cause. God is great!" she said happily.

In the late afternoon, they left earlier, to have something to eat and check out the gigantic malls with too many levels to cover in one day.

"This feels good. It brings back so many memories. I haven't done this movie thing in ages. It feels like in the old times, when I was a teenager with my school friends. These days you hardly get any real, true friends. And life just gets so busy, that we don't always make time for the finer things in life. We just watch movies at home. Thank you for being like a friend and a sister to me, Angel. You bring joy to my life. You bring out the best in me."

"I'm happy to be here for you, my dear." Angel smiled.

They enjoyed the movie. Drove back home.

"You can sleep in tomorrow morning and come in a little later if you prefer. You can call me when I should pick you up, or I can send someone to fetch you."

"No, no. I'm good. I'm good. I'll go with you. I'm so excited. I can't wait to do the perfume thing."

It's chilly, it's February, but because of the sun break, a dozen people were busy outside. Catherine had to drive slowly into the city, because of the congestion and icy conditions. While driving on their way, she asked Catherine about Micah. Catherine doesn't know much about him either, as she only saw him twice.

Angel picked up the sealed boxes out of the boot of Catherine's car.

"Wait here, let me get Gary and Albert to carry the boxes inside."

They greeted everyone.

"Vicky will be just a few minutes, but she'd love you to join her."

"Would you like espressos?" Emily asked.

Emily is counting on her fingers, how many cups to organize. Catherine needed to go into town, to see suppliers.

MASQUED LOVE *BOOK 1*

"Girls, you do what you need to do. I leave you in the capable hands of Vicky. She will guide you along the way. I need to run to appointments. Later!" she shouted.

Vicky had set up a grand spot for the stocks. The parfums were arranged on pretty crystal glass shelves.

"I think we should do a video with you launching, the new perfume collection. The most important factor in our advertising campaign will be to bring out the brands, with an abstract idea of femininity, masculinity, and passion. The brand must be irresistible and must appeal to all the five senses."

"Oh, that is brilliant. I can see why Catherine is so proud of you. You are very professional."

"Thank you." Vicky smiling.

"We can include the video on our existing website. The power of smell. Sensory marketing is a uniquely interactive way to win the audience's attention. So, we do captivated, colorful images and the video, with some, music in the background."

"You think we can finish some of it today? Then we can run the in-store digital signage for display advertising on the televisions, as soon as we are done with the editing. We have another new television with the Screenly Player on the other side installed, as well. This is the best way to promote our brands, since last year. People watch the tv, they see something they like, and ask us for the size and the colors they require. It's like shopping online in-store."

"You get the clothing out and organize the parfums. I will get the equipment ready, and I'll wait for you in the studio. So, you can strut your stuff. You make a perfect model, too."

"Thanks, she laughed loudly. Perfect, yes, of course, I'm on it."

"Ready when you are. These are only a few of the many ranges we have. My hyper-elegant father, always wanted me to join the family business. Although he knows, I'm an independent woman. He thought I'm creative, so this is my chance to express my unique ideas. He admires the way I navigate my way through life, though. He'll be proud of me."

"Yes, I'm proud of you too. There's always room for more, Angel."

The two of them worked well together. They were busy for five days with the ad campaign. With Angel on board, it was extremely overwhelming. She was a great sport, and humorous. It was fun to work with her. Combining the fashion line with the fragrances, was a specifically designed strategy that is carried out across different social media platforms, to increase brand awareness and push up production in sales.

Catherine was astonished to see all the work she's put in. Angel is a versatile person. She has many different skills and great talent.

After working hours, Jacques brought takeaways for dinner.

"Finally, we have completed everything at Micah's new house. He wants to have a housewarming party tomorrow night. Only a few of our cycling friends from the club. We'll get him some gifts tomorrow. I mentioned to him that my sister is at your place. He told me, to bring her along, the more the merrier."

"Your sister's been pretty busy at the boutique. She's like a real breath of fresh air. I wish she could stay with me forever."

"That's Angel, she loves to have her hand in everything. My father always wanted her to work in the family business. Good old Angel had a mind of her own."

"So, did you. Maybe she followed you. You were steered in your own direction."

"That is true."

By late afternoon, Jacques called Catherine on her mobile. He asked her if she could run to the mall and get some gifts for Micah's housewarming. He still had four patients to see before he can leave. Inside the shopping mall, it was warm and light. Soft, snowflakes rained outside.

They walked into different shops and bought pot plants, mirrors, scented candles, and clocks with diamante. She asked the sales assistants to wrap them all up. In the interim, Angel bought some nice toys for the boys, and her precious pumpkin, back home.

After a while, Jacques called to say he was on his way to pick them up.

On their way to Micah, Jacques was clowning around with Angel about what a sweet and gentle man, he is. She just rolled her eyes.

"Excusez Moi, I don't mean to interrupt you, but I particularly don't do long-distance relationships. Friends would be good enough for me, merci!"

Some of the other cycling friends already arrived with their partners. Jacques managed to stop at his place, after work, to pick up some of his own best wines, Armani Pinot Grigio Venezia.

As they walked in, he introduced Catherine and his sister to everyone. The table was set up with all kinds of snacks and assorted finger foods. Some brought homemade cakes. Bottled sparkling waters and juices were on the table. Coffee and tea were served, as well. They all congratulated Micah, on his new house. Everything smelled brand new, as he was touring his guests around the house. Everyone brought awesome housewarming gifts along.

"It's quite a huge house for one person. And now, all you need is a woman to complete and to share your house." Jacques's eyes opened wide, looking in Angel's way.

She gave him a grin look.

"How do you like London? Are you staying here for a while?" Micah asked her, inquisitively.

"I'm not sure, hey. We go to Italy, so probably after the end of the month," she replied.

"That's interesting, what's going on in Italy? You can tell me what you like doing, I can pick you up sometime and show you around town if you want?"

"That would be great. I'll check with Catherine."

"It's the Milan Fashion Week event."

She stared into his eyes for a moment. Catherine saw Angel bounce over to them, with a massive grin on her face.

"Micah is amazing!" she smiles.

"Is that the best you can do?" asked Jacques.

"What do you mean, now? she sighed. Fine, one does not simply grow a conscience with being invited to paint the town red. I'll see, not promising anything, though. Besides, we are very busy at Catherine's."

Since it was a weeknight, some of Micah's friends had a nibble and didn't stay too long. After they all left, Jacques stayed a little longer, to help Micah clear up. He mentioned that he'll make a booking for the four of them for Valentine's dinner at The River Thames.

"Oh, that is fantastic." they all agreed.

They greeted and thanked Micah for a lovely evening.

"Thank you, Jacques, for all the time you have invested in helping me. I couldn't have done it without you. I really appreciate it."

"Anytime, my friend. It's a pleasure. See you tomorrow night. We'll pick you up."

It was Valentine's. They were all dressed up for the Thames dinner cruise with City Cruises. They enjoyed a delectable four-course dinner as they glided through London, taking in the stunning views. Surrounded by the glittering lights of the capital. There was live entertainment and they danced the night away. Lots of couples enjoyed a romantic serenade with spectacular views. It was an unforgettable one. They only got home in the early hours of the morning.

CHAPTER 8

It was work as usual. Everyone was exhausted. Jacques dropped them off at the apartment, kissed her on the lips, and left.

Early Saturday afternoon, after closing time, they were all sitting in the lounge, watching television. Micah knocked at the door. He asked Angel if she would like to go for a drive. She agreed and slipped on something comfortable.

"We won't be long, see you guys later," Angel said.

"Are you asking me or telling me?" Jacques joked.

They all laughed out loud.

They drove through the town. Stopped at many beautiful, iconic places. Had some sushi for dinner and had the best milkshakes at Temptations Milkshake and Ice cream Bar. They strolled through the malls. Enjoying each other's company. Feeling comfortable with each other. There doesn't seem to be any romantic interlude, at least not from Angel's side.

"Thank you for the splendid day out. I really had a good time, Micah."

"Yeah, we should do it again. If you like hiking, we have the best hiking trails, here."

"We could yes, of course. I love hiking. I'm up for any adventure. You just say when, before my time runs out."

"Sure, will do."

It was late when Angel arrived. Jacques was at home. He was helping Catherine with the food. They had light supper with grilled wings and salads.

"Hey, how was your day?"

Jacques pulled her aside in the passage.

"Are you and Micah seeing each other?"

His words were like an allergic reaction and heat instantly build up in her face.

"No," she said emphatically.

"Why would you say that?"

"Just because we were out today? He's your friend. I like him a lot. He's really sweet, but not in a romantic way. All right!" she said in a bitter tone.

She went into her room and slammed the door.

"Don't be so hard on her, Jacques, she's a big girl," Catherine said in the background.

"And what if I did like him that way, would you have had a problem with it?" she shouted from the room.

He knocked at her door. "Angel, Je suis desole. I didn't mean it in a bad way. I'm just looking out for you. I feel responsible for you here."

She opened the door.

"It's fine. Don't worry about it. First, you want to play

matchmaking, then suddenly you worry I might get serious. And he is your friend. I can take care of myself, Jacques. I'm a big girl and I'm responsible. He is a nice sweet guy and I like him as a friend. The feeling is mutual. So, please don't treat me with condescension. Thank you for caring." she said.

Sunday morning Catherine called her mom to say that they won't be coming for lunch, as they will be having a barbeque at her place.

"Are you two, sorted?" Catherine asked Angel.

"Yes, I think he got the message. I'm sorry for the outburst earlier, Catherine."

"No, no don't worry about it. That's normal. I have overprotective brothers, too."

They were busy in the kitchen preparing the meats, steaks, and sausages.

"He loves you. He's just looking out for you. You are his baby sister."

"I know. I was just worried, what if I really fell for Micah? Luckily, we will remain just good friends, hey. Let's just leave it at that."

Jacques and Micah, prepared the wood fire outside, with charcoal briquettes.

The French were particularly good at grilling meat, which they love rare on the inside and crisp on the outside. Jacques was a master when it came to barbeque. As a teenager, this was his Saturday, laid-back evening affair, back in France. Skinny sausages take up the heart of the country. French grill repertoire. The aroma filled the air with the beautiful flavor of the grill.

Angel was setting the table. After adding the veggies and skewers with shrimps and prawns, on the grill, Micah brought with. The potato salad and noodle salad were added to the table with bagels. Catherine also prepared a Greek salad.

"All right, this is the French-style barbeque. Let's eat!" Jacques said.

"Mm, this is really yummy. When last did we have barbeques at home? Since Jacques left. We miss those times." Angel said.

Angel and Micah discussed the hiking trip.

"We have many trails here. I think we'll do the Seaford to East Bourn, the Seven Sisters Cliff Walk. It's a steep drop. Would that be fine for you? The coastal views are breathtaking." Micah explained.

"Yes, yes, of course. I can definitely do it. I'm always up for a challenge."

"My sister comes prepared for anything." they all laughed out loud.

"Why don't you two join us, it'll be fun," Angel asked.

"No, that type of adventure is not for the faint-hearted. I'm not sure how Catherine feels, but I know I can't stand heights."

"Oh, you are chicken!" his sister said.

"No, I'm not chicken. I just don't like heights. Oh yes, Angel, I forgot to thank you for the beautiful gifts you brought me. I simply love it. I love the set of mugs, so cute."

"De rien," she replied.

"So, we leaving on Thursday for Italy. We'll be gone for a while. We going to have to postpone the hiking for another time, Micah. You boys be good in our absence. That's a tall order!" Angel warned.

"Oh, I can't wait. It's going to be awesome. My sister was planning to join us too, but she's tied up. So, it's only me,

Angel and, Emily. Last year at the Spring/Summer event Emily and Amelia joined me. We didn't make the competition, but this time we'll win." Catherine said confidently.

"I can feel it in my bones, and in addition, we have lady luck with us, too. I'm so excited."

"What shall we do during that, alone time, Micah?" Jacques asked jokingly.

"We could cycle." he smiled.

"Yes, I'm first going to my father, spending some time there. I promised them."

Catherine made certain and she kept her word to sort out the Evans before she left for Italy. She went to their house and transferred the three million pounds into Mr. Evans's bank account. She even offered them to settle some of their debt, which they were struggling with. They were appreciating everything Catherine did for them. If only things could have been different when Harold was alive. They wished her good luck and would like to see more of her.

Thursday morning, their bags were packed. They were three ladies, each with two suitcases. Catherine is a light traveler. All her designs were in one of her suitcases. Jacques and Micah dropped them at the airport.

"I'm going to my parents tomorrow. I will spend some time there, and be back by Thursday or the weekend. When are you returning?"

"Either the Tuesday or Thursday. I will let you know."

They greeted and said their goodbyes. After two and a half hours of flight, they landed in Italy. The cab driver drove them to the Palazzo Parigi Hotel, in the heart of the fashion district.

The Milan Women's Fashion Week, strongly emphasized new talent, catwalk shows, and other dedicated events initiatives. Catherine has a selection of emerging eponymous labels to show, too.

In the evenings that followed, Emily and Angel will be strutting their stuff on the catwalk. Plenty of influencers were in attendance and collections spanned, high glamour. There are around seventy shows and presentations of young designers to an international audience. Promoting her elegant designs gave a chance to both the general public and buyers to place orders. Around thirty new designers were showcasing their creations. The Milan Fashion week also collaborates with other countries. Angel and Emily looked like glamorous mannequins. They both could be supermodels. To conclude the season of the week, was the last important event, as the Fashion Hub draws to a close, and was the Awards Ceremony for the special prize. They were competing with many designers.

"And the winner is, Catherine Darcy Evans Designs." the announcement was made.

"Oh, my God. We won, we won!!" Angel said excitedly.

Catherine was all smiles. One of her emerging labels was awarded a special prize by the Italian Chamber of fashion Byers. They were so thrilled, that Catherine ran up to the catwalk, and hugged them both. She called Vicky and Jacques, to tell them the good news. Jacques was spending quality time with his family when she called.

The girls had the time of their lives at the extravaganza. On the last day, they went sightseeing and shopping and only shopped at La Galleria Vittorio Emmanuele 11. The place is very photogenic and luminous, with its magnificent arcades and dome made of glass and iron. They had to take pictures there. On their way back home, Catherine called Jacques to inform him what time they would arrive at the airport.

"Hi love, I missed you!"

"Awe, brother, we're so tired."

"Oh, loud mouth, is back. Congrats on the winnings. Hope you had a glorious time."

"Thank you, darling. Oh yes, we did. It was fantastic. We had great fun. My girls were the best. When did you come home?"

"I came back Sunday evening," he said.

They were all tired of all the glitz and glamour. They dropped Emily off at her house and drove to Catherine's apartment.

"You two can go rest, I will see you tonight." he kissed them both.

After a couple of days, Angel felt a little homesick. She was yearning for her parents.

"I think I need to go home, Catherine. Thank you for everything. You're the best. When I come again, I might stay for good." she laughed.

"You think this coming Sunday will be good to leave? As I want to do the hiking with Micah on Saturday."

"Yes, of course. I need to thank you for all the joy you brought into my life. But I'm going to miss you, though. I got so used to having you here. I love you, Angel. You like a real angel from heaven." Catherine said sadly.

Friday, after Gene and Francois finished their breakfast, they went for their usual morning walk. Francois felt very uneasy. He was short of breath. A couple of minutes later, he was panting and struggling to breathe.

Gene lay him down on the grass patch. She called Arthur and said dad was not well. She thought, she'd call 112 the emergency services as well, just in case, it's serious. And she was right, his breathing became worst until the medics arrived. He was rushed to the medical center. The paramedics revived him. Mom called Arthur again.

Mom: Arthur, your father collapsed. The paramedics are here, they reckoned he had a mild coronary attack. Please inform your brothers.

Arthur: I will, we'll come straight to the hospital. He's going to be fine, Mom.

Mom: I'll stay with him!

She was in a state of panic and cried over the phone. It was late evening when he was stabilized. He was weak. He couldn't speak. He opened his eyes, slightly.

"My wife, I need my wife," he asked softly in a drained voice.

Gene was in the lounge of the hospital, where she was since they brought him in. Arthur and Pierre also waited with her for news.

"Dear God, please, I don't want to lose him." she prayed by herself.

The doctor called Gene into the office and explained to her.

"Mrs. Dupont, your husband had a cardiac arrest, due to there was a blockage on the arteries, so not enough oxygen-rich blood supply, is pumping to the heart."

"Oh, my word, doctor. Is this serious?" she asked in a distressing way.

"We'll have to do surgery on your husband. It will be a small procedure. We make a small incision in his arm, this is called, Angioplasty. We insert a short wire-mesh tube, called a stent, into the artery. The narrowed artery will be stretched open. The stent will be left in place permanently, to allow the blood to flow normally. He needs to eat a heart-healthy diet, but he'll be fine."

"It's rather emergency, we'll push him into theatre in an hour." the doctor explained.

The doctor assured her and gave her peace of mind that everything will be all right and that she could go home and get some rest. He told her that her husband is in good care and she have nothing to worry about. Gene felt a little at ease but prayed every moment, that everything will work out fine for Franc. He is still in the danger zone and the worse is not over yet, but he will heal and be his normal self again. Mom explained to her sons of his condition and they all left to her place.

Back in London, Catherine decided to come with Jacques and Angel to give them support. Angel called Micah to cancel the hiking for Saturday, as an emergency came up. They had to rush home to their father. They took the first available flight to Paris, which was only after midnight. Jacques arranged with Arthur to pick them up at the airport.

Around the early hours of the morning, they arrived and drove to their mom's place. Mom was busy making breakfast in the kitchen. No one was in the mood to eat, but she prepared anyway.

"Mom!" Angel came running in.

"He's going to be fine, right?" she asked in anticipation.

Angel grabbed her and they cried on each other's shoulders.

"Yes, my children. Your father is going to be good again. He is not allowed to get any visitors. The doctor will be doing a small operation on him to the blocked arteries. When he is stable enough and the doctor says he is good to go, he will be discharged in two days. In the meantime, we can all just pray and be strong for each other. Juliette had to take Zoe to her mom. Pierre and Savannah, came around after they dropped off the boys at their cousins. Arthur and Jacques sat on the sofa in the lounge, discussing their father.

Pierre greeted and joined them.

"How're things, Jacques?" Pierre asked.

"All good, very busy though, but dad is my first priority. He was quite fine when I was here. He looked chirpy, and well to me. I took a walk with them one morning, too. He mentioned he needed to talk to me about something, but never managed to. My mind started racing, but I didn't want to ask him. Angel was planning to come home on Sunday, anyway. She was homesick, missing them."

"I sat and ponder last night, why this had to happen to dad," Pierre said.

"Psychological problems, very often underlie, apparently physical disorders," Jacques said.

Pierre could not understand that his father is always in a state of good health and well-being. He always functioned efficiently and effectively. His health just took a sudden, downward spiral recently.

On the porch, mom was sitting with the girls when Savannah walked in. She greeted and looks at Catherine, defiantly. Catherine stood up and took Gene's hand in hers and pull her closer, wrapping her arms around her. Assured her everything will be just fine. Suddenly Savannah lashed out at Catherine.

"Why are you here? What are you even doing here, you're not part of the family!" Savannah yelled.

"Excuse you, Jacques is my boyfriend. When he hurt, I hurt, and so does everyone in this family. You don't just leave people you care about, to go through the pain on their own. Show some compassion, for heaven's sake. If, only your heart could be as big as your mouth." Catherine replied angrily.

"Your narcissistic outbursts will never affect me in any way, whatsoever. Why don't you go back where you came from, since you have an overly inflated sense of your own importance. Show some respect to your husband. My God, these people are in trauma. Get over yourself."

Angel shook her head and walked toward her room. Jacques and his brothers rushed to the porch when they heard the commotion.

"What is going on? Why this uproar, why now?" Jacques asked.

"Oh, go to hell, Jacques!" Savannah said as she walked to the front door and demanded Pierre that they should leave.

He nodded at his brothers, telling them that he will see them later.

Gene was just sitting there in a daze, confused. Not much bothered about her surroundings. All she could think of was Francois.

"What is wrong with Pierre? How could he allow that woman to manipulate him that way?" Jacques asked.

"He will acquiesce, simply because dad is a sick man," Arthur said.

"But he's been doing this all the time. He needs to stand up for himself. This woman is an anarchist, she loves turmoil. She feels no compassion or respect." Jacques continued.

"I have to go into the office, Jacques. Let me know if there's any news about dad."

"Sure, I will stick around, not going anywhere. Staying with mom."

He kissed mom on the head. She's been tearful, most of the morning. Jacques asked her to sit in the lounge with them. Angel saw earlier, that Savannah left with Pierre. She came to join them in the lounge.

"I'm so glad Savannah left, or I would have thrown her out myself," she said in tears.

It was a few agonizing hours, but they all pulled through. You could feel the anxiety, the way it travels through the room, like some kind of mobile energy touching one person and then moving on to the next.

The doctor called to say all went well with the surgery. Francois is in the recovery room. He is still disorientated. If all is good and the doctor is happy with his recovery, then he can be discharged the following day. He will need as much rest as he can, and no exertion.

That was great news. They all felt relief. Jacques called Arthur and Pierre to inform them about their father.

"Let's all go for a drive. Just to get our minds off the worries." Catherine suggested.

"Yes, that's not a bad idea. I'd love to." mom said.

They grabbed their jackets and took a nice long drive through the city and detoured at the Arc de Triomphe. Sitting on the lawn, just talking. Mom said to Jacques that her biggest wish, was for him to return. Home is where the heart is. They needed him there.

Even Angel thought it to be probable.

"This is really good, just being outside and surrounded by nature and being with the ones I love, makes me feel good. I needed this." mom said happily.

"I already feel much better."

They went to eat something light at a restaurant. Arthur called to say they were at the house, but no one's home. Jacques told him they took mom for a drive. She needed to get out. Arthur said it was all good, they will see everyone the next day.

They drove back home. They all settled in to get some rest. Gene and Francois' families called to hear about him. Gene explained to them that he'll be discharged the following day if the doctor sees him fit, but they should keep the visits short. The doctor ordered as much rest as he could. They understood.

CHAPTER 9

In the morning, Gene, Angel, and Catherine prepared his room to convalesce. She took out crispy, white linen, and decorated the room with fresh flowers. Later that afternoon, the doctors gave them the go-ahead that he is good to go home. His three sons picked him up at the hospital. He was really happy to see them. Tears rolled down his cheeks. They kissed him, on both cheeks as real Frenchmen do.

He proudly told the doctor that they were his three rocks. The nurse brought in the wheelchair, but he was adamant and insisted to walk to the car, which was parking right in front of the hospital entrance.

"Today I feel as fit as a fiddle. Let's go home," he said enthusiastically.

"How's your mother doing? God, I missed her. I missed you all. It feels I've been away for a long time."

"Everyone's good. Dad, you need to rest. Please listen to the doctor." they ordered.

"Yeah, yeah! Do what the doctor said."

He stared out by the window, gazing at the high risers outside as they passed by. In the back of his mind, he thought he was going to die. While on the operating table, he thought he wasn't going to make it. His emotions were overwhelming. Tears continued to roll down his face. As they pulled up into the driveway, everyone was waiting outside. Savannah also arrived on her own.

"Hi everyone." Savannah greeted as if nothing happened.

"This one is a real split personality. She better behave herself." Angel said.

Francois held his wife, tight. They wept together. It was a sad moment. He was so happy to be home. Angel laid next to him in bed. The kids were all around their Pepe.

"I'm so sorry I wasn't here for you, dad. I'll never leave you again." Angel kissed him.

"I understand my girl, I'm just glad that you're here at home."

In the evening the family members, came in and out to see Francois. Savannah kept to herself. She played with the kids in the playroom. Catherine was helping, Juliette in the kitchen, serving some juice and tea to the people. As she walked down the passage, her eyes fell on Raoul. The guy, she spotted in the restroom with Savannah. Raoul is married to Jacques's cousin, Yvonne.

Yvonne's mom and Gene, are sisters. They all grew up together as kids, so they are very close. Catherine called him outside.

"You have no shame showing your face here. What are you doing here, anyway? Coming to tell, Pierre how sorry you are about his father?" Catherine demanded.

"Look at you. Who the hell do you think you are? You only passed by in this family recently, and you want to pass demands. Don't you patronize me, woman! Never you mind, look the other way." he said defensively.

She just gave him a stern look and walked back inside. In the meantime, Raoul sends Savannah a text message to tell her about Catherine trying to reprimand him. He warned Savannah that Catherine is acting in a presumptuous way and that she must be careful.

Late in the evening, all the visitors left. The house was quiet. The atmosphere was somber. Everyone was around in the lounge, and in the kitchen, but the air of melancholy filled the house. Francois was alone in his room. He felt uneasy. What if he won't make it through the night. He gathered all his thoughts together. Thoughts he had in the hospital. Somehow, he just couldn't rest. He needed to get some important matters off his chest. He asked Gene to call in the sons. He wanted to have a word with them. Gene asked him if he couldn't wait until the next day. He said to her it's very important. They were all in the lounge when their mother called them to say, their dad wanted to see them. As they walked in, they were uncertain what to expect.

"My sons, I love you all equally. In my condition, as you all know, my life hangs on a thread. You never know what tomorrow brings. I might not be here tomorrow, so I need to have this heart-to-heart with all of you. Arthur and Pierre are both my right arms in the company. I am equally very proud of all three of my sons. Jacques had his own endeavors he needed to fulfill. However, I wished every day that he could join his brothers in the empire, we have built together. I have recently found embezzlement in the company's financials. Pierre, as you know that Savannah is working on the accounts. Arthur is fully aware of the situation."

"Oh my God, why wasn't I told," Pierre asked angrily.

"Are you accusing Savannah of theft, dad? How certain are you? Do you have any evidence, dad?" he contradicted.

"We all working together on this matter to get to the bottom of it. We got in special auditors to check everything, but this will take time. Time is something I don't have much of. Time is of the essence. After delving into this matter and doing my own checks, I am certain, it must be Savannah, therefore I had to change my will. Pierre, I have left eighty percent of your shares in Jacques's name. In the event things don't work out between you and Savannah, then she cannot claim your shares."

"That is not fair, dad. That is absurd! Jacques is not even part of the company. Why Jacques, why not Arthur? No offense, Jacques. What's going on?" Pierre was by now, very upset.

"I have a clause in the will, stating Jacques will pay you, your dues, should anything have to happen to me. You are all equally the main stakeholders of the company. And, also all three of you, have to promise me that you will always take care of your mother and sister. You three brothers have to stand strong together, and never forget your family values."

"Yes, of course, dad. They will remain our priorities. That is something you never have to worry about." they all agreed.

"Pierre, I know you are upset and I'm so sorry to break the news to you this way. It is a rather sensitive matter. I drove past the school en route to the office, a couple of weeks back. I spotted Savannah's car. I pulled over as I saw she was talking to a man. I couldn't see who he was, as I was parking from a distance. They got into his car and stayed there for almost half an hour. Until the school dismissed. She got out and they looked too cozy together and they kissed. I'm not sure how anyone would react to that. Why did they kiss? Something must be cooking. This is why I have my eye on her and have suspicion and doubts about her. I haven't told a soul, not even your mother. You are her husband, only you will know."

Pierre was now very distraught. This is a lot to take in, in one shot. Arthur and Jacques put their hands on his back and stood by his side. "This is a difficult situation, Pierre. We understand this is hard to fathom. We are here for you, brother. We'll never let you down."

"This is why Pierre. I'm doing this to protect you. You don't even look surprised. It seems like you are aware of, or you surmised an affair." dad said.

"Yes, she has been acting strangely for many months, now. We sleep in separate rooms. She claims the boys won't sleep alone. They get nightmares. At first, I was inclined to think, she is seeing someone. Then I was hoping it was something else going on. It crossed my mind, but you have confirmed it for me, dad, and I'm very thankful for it. Even the embezzlement. That explains, her always snooping around on my laptop. She was always eavesdropping. I never thought anything of it, as she is working in the accounts department. What is there to hide. And, also the company's credit card. But why I don't understand. I give her everything. Is she not happy with me? Is it me, am I the problem?" he started to get emotional.

"She's a real gold digger, that woman," Arthur said.

"I'm going to speak to her tonight, and I will decide on

the way forward. I have to think of my boys, too." Pierre said tearfully.

His brothers comforted him. They kissed their father.

It was late. The kids fell asleep. Savannah was sitting alone in the kitchen, having coffee. Angel was already gone to bed. Arthur and Juliette took Zoe and went home. Pierre and Savannah carried the boys to the car and left. Mom settled in after giving Francois his medications.

"Franc, is everything okay? That was a long talk."

"All is good. I feel much better now. We'll talk tomorrow. Thank you for everything, my beautiful wife. I love you dearly."

Jacques and Catherine were still in the lounge, watching television. Jacques pulled her closer to him and whispered in her ear.

"I love you, thank you for being here for me and all of us during our trying times," he said.

"I love you, more. You mean the world to me, Jacques."

It was quiet in the car. Pierre couldn't wait to get home to settle the boys in. He wanted to confront her right now. He tucked them in himself and closed the door of the room. He asked her to sit down.

"What's your problem, I need to take a shower."

"Not until you tell me, how long is this sordid affair been going on. Who is he? Why?"

"What affair are you talking about?" she tried to deny.

"Oh, please don't give me more lies and deceit."

She tried to lie her way out of it, but it was written all over her face. Pierre started to work himself up and raised his voice. He felt like smacking her through her face but had second thoughts. She's not worth it. He is a real man,who follows the rules, and never raise your hands to a woman. She sat there with indiscretion, showing no remorse.

"Who is he, I asked?" he yelled.

"Raoul!" she started to cry crocodile tears.

"Raoul, Yvonne's husband? Wow, you sure know how to pick them. What a disgrace you are. You have shamed my family. How do I look Yvonne in the eyes, again? She's like a sister to me. They were at my father's tonight. What a jerk. He still spoke to me in the meantime he's screwing my wife."

He held his hands over his head. He cannot believe this is happening to him. Savannah's thoughts moved to Catherine. She's the only one who knows. She wouldn't dare ask Pierre, how he knew. She blamed everything on Pierre. That he was always occupied and busy with family ties.

"How did it all start? Did you just fall into his loving arms, or just jumped into his bed by mistake? This was probably since the time you started to sleep in the boys' room. You used your children as an excuse for your deceit. Do you love him? He's a married man, a father of kids. He's my cousin's husband, for crying out loud. What do you expect from him, to leave his wife for you? Or do you just like your bread buttered on both sides. How could you do this to me? I'll never forgive you for this."

He went into his room and slammed the door.

It seems like his world is falling apart. The humiliation and grief she caused him. When your wife cheats and blames you for the cheating, she is not only unfaithful but dishonorable, as well. She betrayed his trust. If it was another man, he could handle it, but it's amongst the family, which makes it even harder.

He needs to ride those emotional waves until it passes. This had been the loneliest, moment of his life. All he can do now is stare blankly. This is so much to absorb. He cannot think straight. He needs to keep strong for his boys and especially for his father's sake. Life has many ways of testing a person's will, either by having nothing happen at all or by having everything happen all at once.

Pierre feels destroyed. His heart is broken into a million pieces. He is the soft-spoken one. Everyone knew his marriage was a sham. His silence was always just another word for his pain and hurt. He wondered if she really loved him. His mind is in such turmoil, he didn't know what his thoughts were.

Savannah couldn't wait to get her hands on Catherine. She couldn't fall asleep. Her guilt was consuming her. If she had a conscience, she would have apologized to her husband.

In the morning Pierre took Jules and Lois to school. He woke them, and gave them breakfast, as he does every morning. It was time to drop them off at school. This was the moment he could meet up with Raoul. Perhaps it won't be a good idea. Not at a school. Savannah probably warned him, that the cat was out of the bag. Pierre was thoughtful about all this. What if he should see Raoul at school. Now that he had heard fairly authoritatively, that Savannah was in an extramarital affair. Maybe this is it. The marriage was over. He kissed his boys and got into his car and drove off. Today was totally different. He took a shower and left for the office. No words were spoken. Savannah stayed at home. She was either too embarrassed and ashamed or felt a great deal of inferiority. She didn't know what to expect. Mid-morning, she goes to her in-laws' house to check on her father-in-law.

But mostly, she had it with Catherine and wanted to have a word with her.

As she entered, she greeted everyone. Francois was still asleep at that time. The medication made him drowsy. She realized that she might not have another chance to do this. Some family members came in and out to see Francois. Some said that they would come later. Some waited in the lounge and spoke to Gene. Savannah followed Catherine to the kitchen. Pretending to have a glass of water.

"How could you be so mean? Is this your way of first getting me out of the way, then worming your sorry ass into this family?" Savannah was boiling with anger.

"Excuse me, what do you mean by that?"

"Oh, please, don't act like you are all innocent. You just waited for the right moment to tell Pierre. I should have known. You want to destroy my life. Well, you have succeeded. Congratulations. Do you have any idea who your lover boy really is? I didn't think so!"

By now they were at each other's throats. Savannah started to raise her voice and yelled.

"Ask him, you stupid woman. Your dear lover boy killed your husband in the accident."

Catherine turned white from the shocking news. Jacques and Angel rushed to the kitchen when they heard the racket in front of the family.

"Is this true, Jacques? Is it true?"

"Catherine, I can explain."

She ran out of the kitchen, went into the room to grab her bag, and left as fast as she could. She was in tears.

"Catherine, wait, please. This is not what it seems."

"Leave me alone, Jacques."

She called a cab to drive her to the airport. The next available flight was only in the next few hours. She had no choice but to hang around at the airport. Her mobile phone was switched off.

Jacques screamed at Savannah.

"What have you done? You slut!"

Jacques took Angel's car and drove around the neighborhood to see if he could find Catherine. Angel was so disgusted at Savannah, that she asked her to leave and never come back.

Jacques ended up at the office. Pierre was busy with a client when Jacques entered. He waited. He was all flustered. Pierre could see Jacques looked devastated.

"She left me. Catherine left me," he said sadly.

"What happened, brother?"

"Savannah told her about the accident. She just stormed out. I don't even know where she is. How did Savannah know? Have you told her? I only spoke to you about it."

"No, never. I swear to you, Jacques. She must have overheard or listened in on our conversation. Dear God, I just remembered now, I was busy shaving when you called and I switch my phone to a speaker phone. She must have listened in. What is it about this woman? She's turning our life upside down. I'm planning to file for a divorce. I can't stand that woman."

"I don't blame you, Pierre. I would have done the same. You made the right choice, no doubt about it."

"To put the cherry on top, guess who is the guy, she's having an affair with?"

"I have no clue. I can't even think straight now, Pierre."

"Raoul, Yvonne's husband."

"You joking. Are you serious?"

"It came straight from the horse's mouth."

Arthur walked in and sat on the edge of the sofa, and asked what came from the horse's mouth. They told him the awful news.

"Good gracious. What is next? With Savannah, you can expect anything. She couldn't have chosen a better time. Savannah is a master of disaster." Arthur said in dismay.

"I'm going to leave her. I want a divorce as soon as possible. I want her out of my life."

"Juliette called me to say what had happened earlier. You go and find Catherine, Jacques. That is a real classy woman. No offense, Pierre, but they are like chalk and cheese."

"Oh, I know." Pierre agreed.

"Juliette is also one in a million," Jacques said.

"I never knew or realized that Catherine was the wife of the deceased. I was already head over hill in love with her when I saw his pictures at her apartment. I froze and panicked. It was Christmas time. I didn't want to spoil the vibe. I wouldn't even have known how to say this to her. Then I called Pierre and he suggested I leave it and don't say anything. She hates me now."

"I can assure you, Jacques. That woman really loves you. Give her time to calm down. It's been a shock to her. In her mind, this feels like you are a coward and you didn't tell her. It was in a harsh manner, Savannah told her. With a love that is strong, nothing and no one can tear it apart. It was an accident. It was never your fault. She will eventually understand. True love knows no reason, no boundaries, no distance. Love breaks down boundaries. Love accepts and embraces the boundaries. It has the sole intention of bringing people together to a time called, forever. If you are meant to be together, you will end up with each other. As for you Pierre, you do what is best for you and your children. We have your back. So, let's get back to work." Arthur gave them some brotherly guidance.

Jacques went back home. Angel was in a state too.

"Jacques, how can you let go of something so good? Why couldn't you tell her about this terrible thing? We all know it was an accident. She would have understood." she said stricken.

Jacques just went to sit in the lounge, overwhelmed by all this.

"Jacques, talk to me, I'm your sister, you have no closer friend than me."

"I know. We have to sort out what to do first. Give her some time to think. Give her some space. She's upset. The way Savannah brought it on her, was like I literally killed her husband." Jacques said.

"I'm just glad, dad was still asleep when all this played out earlier. This would just have disrupted his recovery." Jacques added.

"If you don't hear anything from her, I will fly over to her. At least I can console her. For the past few months, I grew attached to her. I love her too Jacques. We've just started working together so nicely. I don't want you to lose her." Angel said.

"I promise I will get her back, even if I should climb the highest mountain, I'll do it for her," Jacques said in a certain voice.

Catherine arrived home early in the evening. Her heart

is shattered. She looked at the pictures of her husband. She cried non-stop for a moment.

"Oh, my dear Harold, I'm so sorry. Please forgive me. How could this happen to me?"

She sat down in the lounge, keeping a frame with Harold's photo, in her arms. She cried herself to sleep that night. She woke up, hoping this was only a bad dream. She had to pinch herself, to realize that this is all for real.

She took a long shower, washing all her tears and pain away. Despite feeling awful, and the difficulties she's facing, she dressed up in blue jeans, a sequined top, and her diamante pumps. It was a nice sunny day, but still a crisp chill in the air. She took her jacket with her. She pulled out her car and went for a drive through the city. Next to her were enormous, double-length buses, painted in bright red, that were so tightly packed with people, that she wondered how they breathed. The city was virtually gridlocked, but never before had a traffic jam looked so good. Catherine didn't mind. She just had to clear her head. She had no idea what to make of all this. One thing is for sure, she knows that she loves Jacques, dearly. Her memory promptly conjured up the sensation of Jacques's arms around her. Then she tried to suppress her thoughts. Everything merged into one, the past and the present. A small lump of fear began to grow in her heart.

They did agree that they always wanted to be together, and live their dreams, despite any obstacles that might come their way. Angel tried numerous times to call her. Her phone was off, completely. Her phone was still in her bag. Battery dead. She wouldn't touch the phone as she knew Jacques would call her. She felt empathy towards him. Why didn't he mention it to her? Maybe, she would not have fallen so madly in love with him. What if he told her? How, would she have reacted to it? All the confusion drove her mind crazy.

She parked her car and went for a long walk. A walk down memory lane. This was where Harold took her when they had a picnic on the grass. Many people were sitting on the lawn. Children were playing. Some were with their parents, some with their grandparents. A little girl brought her a flower. She cried and gave the small girl a tight hug.

"Thank you, my sweetheart."

A pretty flower from this pretty little girl made her smile.

When the lady with the little girl came up to her, a while later, she said.

"I can see you hurting, my child. Everything will work out just fine."

She rubbed her hand over Catherine's head.

"Thank you, Ma'am."

She felt so good after this lady's special touch. On her way home, she decided to stay indoors. She wanted to be alone. Life is unfair. After charging her phone, she saw over two hundred missed calls from Jacques. There was also a texted message from Angel. She read it.

'Please don't leave my brother. You two are a match made in heaven. I'm flying over to you soon. Please don't shut me out. All my love, Angel.'

The weekend continued to be a tearful one.

Meanwhile back in Paris, Jacques was struggling to come to terms that he had lost the love of his life. Jacques was like a lost soul without Catherine. He couldn't eat, he couldn't sleep, he was just restless. He drove around in the city, playing the song, Lady, by Lionel Richie, over and over, in his car. At first, he didn't feel like going back to London. He decided to get a Locum Tenens, to stand in for him while he was away. At the moment, he doesn't know where he is on or off. And he is in Paris for his parents' sake, to be there for them.

CHAPTER 10

It's Monday morning. Catherine needed to face the staff at work. It's a rather difficult task. She couldn't face anyone. Catherine called Vicky to say, she wasn't feeling well, she was staying in bed for a couple of days. Her few days continued for a whole week. One morning, her doorbell rang. It was Vicky at her door.

"Hullo, stranger. Oh, my gosh, you look like hell."

"Hi, Vicky."

"It seems like you don't have a boutique to run anymore. Your phone is off, I had to come to see for myself, what is wrong. What's troubling you, my dear?"

"Vicky, to make a long story short, Jacques and I broke up. It's too painful. I don't feel like talking about it."

"Oh, no! That is so sad. All right, I will spare you the details. I just know that you two will get back together again. Whatever the problem is, it will work out on its own. Let me give you the good news. We have orders from five big fashion couture houses, who want to buy the parfums. They have huge orders, for both ladies and gents. And the sales have skyrocketed, since our videos with Angel showing the new lines on the in-store latest marketing."

"Oh, my word, Vicky. You're the best. What would I do without you? I know I can rely on you with my life. Please explain to the girls about my dilemma. I just need to pull myself together. It's not easy for me to give up someone I love with all my heart and soul. I'll be back shortly. You are capable of handling everything. I need to get my act together."

"Sure, sure. Whenever you are ready. Everything will be just fine, you'll see." Vicky gave her the thumbs up.

On Wednesday early morning, she took a drive to her parents. Jacques continued to call her.

"Oh dear, James, look who is here! This is strange. Shouldn't you be at work?"

She held them tight and just burst out in tears. All she said was that she missed them so much, especially after missing out on a whole lot of Sunday lunches with them. She stayed the whole day with them. She was telling them about Jacques's father, who had a mild heart attack, and that he is recovering now. She said she was also in Paris to support the family. She didn't say much further.

Of course, her mother and father, know their daughter, as any parent would. She couldn't fool them. They knew she was hurting. She left without saying anything, more.

In the weeks that followed, Jacques went back to London to check on work. He kept by himself, from work, back home. No contact with anyone, not even his close friend, Micah. Even the receptionist lady could see, that Jacques was not himself.

Two weeks later, Angel decided to go to Catherine. She made sure her father was all good. She arranged with Micah to pick her up at the airport. On their way home, Angel told Micah the whole story.

He was shocked. He knew about an accident that Jacques was involved in, but he didn't know it was Catherine's husband. Catherine was not at her apartment when they pulled up. They decided to drive around the city and then to the boutique.

Catherine was on her way to the Evans. She rang the doorbell. They opened the door and were surprised to see Catherine in that state.

"Oh, my dear, what's wrong?"

"I'm so sorry for everything. I loved Harold, so much and I have a special place in my heart for him where he shall remain," she said emotionally.

"Yes, we know you loved our son, dearly. We miss him terribly."

"I kept my promise when I said I will grant you the money on behalf of your son. I need to ask you about the accident. I was devastated when the accident happened. All I remember was that I lost my husband. I don't remember how or what happened. I was too distraught and traumatized. For me it was like, his time was up and God called him back. What really happened that night?" she asked.

"Well, there was a police report. As I can remember vaguely. Harold was crossing the street. It was meters away from the pedestrian. The road was wet and slippery from the snow. Harold just, blindly, ran over the road in front of a car. He probably didn't see the car. It was a dark BMW. The driver hit him as he braked and swerved. This made the car skid on the road. Harold's body was flung to the other side of the road. The driver rushed out of his car to get to him, but then another car drove over Harold. This was how he succumbed to his injuries. That was what the police report said and the autopsy said that he was still alive after the first knock. The driver was traumatized by the accident. Knowing that he couldn't save the injured, in time. I have heard that he needed counseling after this happened. This was an accident. It was no homicide case. There were witnesses on the scene, who saw it happen. That was God's plan for him, my dear. You have to move on and accept that Harold is gone." Mr. Evans explained.

Catherine cried, bitterly. They consoled her.

"The problem is that I have recently discovered, that the man I am in love with, was the driver in the dark car, who knocked Harold down. We broke up two months ago. How can I love another man who was the cause of my husband's death?"

"Oh, my dear Lord. Is his name Jacques Dupont?" Mr. Evans asked.

"Yes, I never knew he was the man involved in the accident." she cried uncontrollably.

"The man is innocent. I'm sure there must be an explanation on his side." Mrs. Evans said.

"Please speak to him and hear him out. You are a young and beautiful woman. You have your whole life ahead of you. Your journey with our son ended, when he died. Harold would have wanted you to be happy. You hold him close within your heart." Mr. Evans advised her.

"We don't know what lies ahead of us in our journey in this

life. God is in control of our lives. If you love this man, go and find him." Mrs. Evans further advised her.

"Thank you, thank you so much."

She felt much better after hearing this. Still, in a weepy state, she stood up and hugged them both.

"All the best to you. We wish you a very happy life. You are always welcome in our home. Please do come regularly. We would like to see more of you."

"I will I promise. I feel much better now. Thank you once again, for the parental guidance." she smiled.

She drove straight to the boutique and found Angel and Micah there. They both embraced in each other's arms, very emotional.

"Oh, my God Catherine. Are you okay?"

"I would feel exactly the same way as you do. I don't blame you. I missed you so much."

They left the boutique to go to the apartment.

"Have you heard from Jacques, yet? He's been running around like a headless chicken. Please speak to him, Catherine. It was an accident. He suffered enough. At the time of the accident, he was so traumatized, that he needed counseling. I promise you my brother is innocent, and he loves you very much."

Catherine agreed to speak to him. She told Angel she came from the Evans. They had a good heart-to-heart. Jacques was also in town. Angel contacted him to meet at Catherine's place. On his way there, Angel and Micah left.

When she saw Jacques, she held him tight in her arms and cried.

"Catherine, I'm so sorry about all this. I could never find the right moment to tell you about this. This was not something simple and easy to tell you. I was afraid of losing you. I just couldn't take the risk. I love you too much. I missed you."

"Everything is all good. I understand."

They kissed and made up. Sitting in her lounge, he explained to her.

"When I saw you sitting at the table at the restaurant that first night, I couldn't take my eyes off you. You were alone in your own world and that I found strange. I was captivated by your beauty, and you just captured my heart. Even if you did not have a puncture that night, I was still coming out to approach you. I genuinely fell in love with you. I never knew he was your husband." Jacques explained.

"I understand."

"While I was waiting for you before we went to your parents for Christmas lunch, I saw his picture in your lounge. I panicked and went to my car to call Pierre. His phone was on loudspeaker and Savannah listened in on our call. My father saw her kissing a man outside, in the open, at their kids' school. That night my father wanted to see all of us, he told Pierre about the affair amongst other things."

"Wow, so she must have thought it was me. The night of your mother's 60th birthday, I saw her making out with your cousin's husband in the restrooms. Caught him with his pants down. I gave him a stern warning that night at your father's house when he was discharged from the hospital. Speaking of your father, how is he doing?"

"He is much better, taking it easy. He followed the doctor's orders and rested. He is up and about but still has to take it easy, no overexertion. He feels on and off. He's definitely not the man he used to be. I spent a lot of time with them. They were also my comfort when you left me. Pierre is also distraught. He is busy with divorce proceedings."

"That is so sad. What did your dad say about our breakup?"

"Oh, my father was all good. He said he knows everything will work out for the best, and that he just knew we'll get back together again. Mom was upset at one stage, but she was also certain that we are made for each other and that nothing can break up a love that is so strong. Please never let anything come between us ever again?"

They spoke for hours and made wild passionate love. It's been a long time. The make-up was a thousand times more intense than before. Making love to Catherine was wild and extremely gratifying. The foreplay and intimacy heightened their state of arousal to the highest level. They declared their love for each other.

When Angel returned, she was happy to see the two back together again.

She invited Micah to spend some time with her in Paris, whenever he was free. Angel thanked Catherine for her courage.

"Thank you for your words of wisdom, and everything you have done for me and your brother. You have a heart of gold. Thank you, darling."

"Awe, it's a pleasure!"

"Vicky told me about the big order that came through. I'm so thrilled. We'll sort that out when I'm coming back again. I was just here for one important mission. My mission was accomplished."

Angel left the following morning, as she wanted to be

there for Pierre during his divorce proceedings. And, also for Lois and Jules. They are kids, but they can sense the trouble between their mommy and daddy.

Pierre and Savannah argued most of the time. He always knew that their marriage was toxic, but he gave his whole life to her. He tried his best to please her. Her priorities have changed. She overburdened him with her demands. There was no more love and care coming from Savannah. His family knew that he had a troubled marriage, but always overlooked things for his sake. Sometimes he blamed himself, but then it seemed impossible, as he knew he truly contributed his life to this marriage. The humiliation was more of real hurt to him than the breakup. Maybe that was the best thing happening to him. To rid himself of all this pain and resentment. To put an end to it.

"You know I had to hear from my father, about your affair. He saw you at school, flirting and smooching with Raoul, out in the open."

Savannah appeared shocked, but then, again she didn't have a real conscience, anyway. She found it to be a pleasure to destroy people. She hated to see Jacques and Catherine and Arthur and Juliette so happy together. So now she realized, that it was Franc who told Pierre and not Catherine. But she didn't care.

"Just after Jules was born, my feelings changed towards you. We just grew apart, I guess I don't love you anymore, Pierre. I stopped loving you for a while. The marriage failed a long time ago. And I have tried."

"You have tried? You have never tried, you just carried on, by controlling me and blaming me for everything, until you thought having a side-kick lover, will solve everything and you stayed with me for convenience, sake, and security. You never really loved me. But, it's time to move on and go our separate ways."

Pierre filed for divorce from Savannah a few weeks ago. They wished to part amicably and to come to a settlement agreement as to the terms of the divorce. The attorney drafted the necessary documentation, which included the assets and custodial maintenance of the children. The documents were signed. He had an antenuptial agreement in place. His father was not aware of it. This was why he wanted to protect Pierre from Savannah's greedy claws. His father knew his marriage would end up in divorce.

They both have custody of the boys. The company auditors confronted her about the fraud. Everything pointed in her direction. She had no choice and admitted to the fraud. She could not account for where all the money was. This was a big loss to the company. Pierre and his father decided not to press charges against her, as she was the mother of his boys. The whole affair with Raoul and Savannah also gave rise to an acrimonious controversy in the family.

Raoul ended his relationship with Savannah and reconciled with his wife. They went to a marriage counselor. Pierre and Savannah parted amicably, especially because of the boys. Savannah was declared the bitch and ostracized by the family. She was a sore loser, which was her own execution.

Angel told her mom that everything was sorted and good with Jacques and Catherine. Mom was contented to hear all worked out for the best for the two of them. Mom was also very occupied with her husband, so she didn't worry much about Jacques and Catherine's issues. And she was certain, they would sort it out. She just knew that they would get back together again.

Angel was so excited when she was telling her father about the big orders for the parfums. He was overjoyed.

"I knew you could do it, darling. You just have it in you. Everything you touch turns into gold. You make me so proud. I love you, my darling. That is why I wanted you to be a part of the company. You sort the parfum orders out with your brothers." dad said happily.

"I got it from my Pappa." she smiled.

As time passed, Francois got weaker and weaker. Jacques spent more time with his father than before. Gene was too distraught about her husband's on and off bouts of illness, she could not think clearly. His health deteriorated. She knew he was leaving her. The thought alone left her in excruciating pain.

Four months later, on a warm sunny morning, on the fifth day of July, Francois sadly passed away of massive heart failure. He was a real fighter. The night before. He spoke to his beloved wife about the beautiful life they had together. How much he loved her. He repeatedly said he was tired. Everyone was around him. All his children, and his grandchildren. They knew he was leaving them, but not so soon. Angel nodded off next to him, laying in his arms. Jacques and Catherine flew in two days before. He was in constant endurance of pain. He was suffering. When he passed, they somehow felt relieved to know he was out of his pain. He was on oxygen for over a month. Gene couldn't stand to see her lively, vivacious husband in that state. It was painful. The whole family was around when he breathed out his last breath. He looked peacefully and youthful.

The doctor was called to issue a death certificate. The coroner arrived, a while later and the boys got the body removed to the mortuary. The funeral arrangements were made. Gene's head was complicated with grieving. Juliette and Angel were both very sad, but they had the daunting task of do the funeral arrangements with the funeral director. His wish was to have a burial. Gene chose a black suit and white shirt with a tie. Francois was a very neat, classy, and sought-after man. He was a pure and powerful man, always serious about life, and sophisticated, so the family decided on a black casket with a glossy finish. Angel arranged the flowers. White flowers represent honor and peace, and the colored flowers expressed gentleness, respect, sympathy, love, and strength. Francois was a man full of personality. She posted the details of the funeral on social media. Gene called the families from both sides.

Angel and Juliette also organized the Chapel, the food, and the burial site. Micah arrived the day before the funeral. He needed to be there for Angel and to give his condolences to the family. The day of the funeral was on the fourteenth day of July. It was also Bastille Day. Francois loved to celebrate the festival of Bastille Day with his family. This was an annual event and he took his children since they were young kids.

They watched the lavish military parade, displaying French power on the Champs-Elysees. In the evening, beautiful firework displays filled the skies and people would dance to the Le Bal des Pompiers. This was the saddest day for the family.

The funeral procession was underway. The pallbearers carried the casket into the church. The minister doing the service was Francois's longtime friend. Minister Raphael Fleur Richelieu. There was a big blown-up picture of Francois, by the casket. Two hours before the service, there was viewing for the family and friends, who wanted to pay their last respects. Jacques was the spitting image of his father. The dress code was black. The song Ave Maria played. He loved that song.

The Saint-Germain-des -Pies Cathedral was packed to capacity. He was a widely known man and loved by everyone. Angel with her three brothers, stood in front to read the eulogy.

'Hi, everyone. I am Angelique Dupont. My brothers Arthur, Pierre, and Jacques, are the children of one great man, Francois Dupont. I want to thank you all for coming out today to celebrate my father's beautiful life. Although today is going to be a very hard day, I want to take this time to remember and honor the special memories, I had with my dad. My father was an incredible person. He touched lives. He was not only the best role model to all his children, but he also wanted to give back to the world and help others in need. He was hard working and the kindest and most gentle, man I have ever known. He raised me and my brothers, to be strong, confident, take risks, and always believe in ourselves. I don't know how long it will take me to grieve this tremendous loss. My father was the most important person in our lives, and we feel heartbroken, to no longer have him here with us. He's smiling down on us. His memory will forever carry on.'

Tears rolled down her face.

Gene was sitting in between Juliette and Catherine. They were very sad and in deep grief.

Funeral hymns were sung, Guide Me O Thou Great Redeemer. The celebrant presided over the memorial service. He did his tribute, reading his obituary about Francois. The minister was a close friend of the deceased. Francois had given regular charity to the churches in his area, every month, for many years. After the prayer service ended, and the memorial service was so beautiful, the hearse was ready. The pallbearers together with Arthur, Pierre, and Jacques, carried the coffin to the hearse to be transported to The Pere Lachaise Cemetery, which was close to his home. Another prayer was read at the burial site before the casket was lowered. The grandchildren dropped their favorite toys and small teddies onto the casket for their beloved Pepe. Angel and everyone else dropped soil, flowers, and notes onto it. The family and friends were informed about the reception after the funeral service, at the hall of the cathedral. Lamb, rice, and bread were served.

The blessings of the charity, go to the deceased.

"Rest in peace our dear father. We will miss you every day and you will forever be in our hearts." Arthur said sobbing.

It was a beautiful funeral. It was amazing to see how many people knew him.

The loss happened in a moment, but its aftermath lasts a lifetime. There wasn't a dry eye in the house the next day. It felt empty, like something or someone was missing.

Gene was very quiet. She accepted the fact that he was gone forever and will never come back. All she has left of him were their memories. The legacy of character and faith, he left behind in his children.

Micah had to leave that morning. He greeted Angel and gave her a big tight hug.

"I can only imagine how you feel. I'll be here for you if you needed to talk or just need someone to listen. It was a beautiful memorial and sent off."

Micah recorded the whole service. Jacques and Catherine decided to stay a while longer, to comfort his mother.

"If you needed to go back to London, it will be okay, Catherine," Jacques said.

"No, never. You are in deep pain. I want to be here for you, my love."

He got emotional and cried on her shoulder. Pierre was also in a state, especially after all the difficulties he's been through the past few months. He was inconsolable. He found it difficult to come to terms that his father is no longer there for him. Pierre and his two little boys stayed at his mother's house to comfort each other. Arthur and Juliette also took turns sleeping over at Gene's house. Someone had to be there for her all the time. Arthur was a strong man, but at times he would break down and have a good cry. It's still very raw. Like an open wound. They all grieved in their own way. They move through their tragedies and challenges together. To them, it's like their father never left. It had not sunk in yet.

CHAPTER 11

After a few weeks, Jacques and Catherine went back to London. Arthur continued with the running of the company. Francois's, last will were read out after two months. Arthur was the responsible one, the more stable one, of the brothers. His father appointed him as the executor of his last will and testament. After Pierre told his father about the antenuptial agreement, he had in place and when his divorce proceedings were finalized, his father did amendments to his will. Half of his estate was left to Gene and the other half was left to be shared in equal parts to his four children. That includes all his assets. There were three educational policies for his grandchildren Lois, Jules, and Zoe worth one million pounds each, which they are entitled to receive, only when they reach the age of eighteen.

Jacques called his mother daily, sometimes a few times per day. She made him believe that she was fine, but she wasn't coping. Angel had to go through her own grief. Sometimes she regrets, being away for long and not being by her father. She watched short video clips she made with him. She listened to his voice notes, which he left on her phone. But she knows she was a good daughter to him, and she knows she made him proud. Thoughts like that, kept her going. Micah called her every day. The caring coming from a friend she only knows recently was overwhelming for her. She appreciated the caring.

Angel called her brothers every day, as their mother showed signs of depression. Juliette also spent time at Gene and Angel either in the mornings or the afternoons. It was two months after Francois passed on. The atmosphere was somber for a long time. Gene stayed in a daze. She watched their memorable videos of their younger days. She had a box of hard drives. She flipped through it which was marked, wedding day, Arthur, Pierre, Jacques, and Angelique. Videos of when each child was born. Their children's birthdays, their holidays. She started with the wedding day and how young and handsome Francois was. She saw a lot of Jacques in him. She watched their celebrations throughout their life, on television. She watched her 60th birthday celebration. And then she moved on to the memorial service.

She, kept busy, watching those in the months that passed. She never went out. Only when they visited their father's grave and put fresh flowers on. She didn't have a decent meal for days and this caused her to lose a lot of weight. Sometimes she goes into disbelief and denial. She gets illusional, talking to her husband as if he's around. She would take two coffees for her and Franc to the porch. She also gets angry for no reason. Arthur and Pierre stopped by every day, at different times. Angel was sitting with Arthur, having coffee and snacks on the porch, one morning.

"Arthur, I think we should call a family meeting. As soon as Jacques comes back. Mom asked for him every day. I think since she's been watching the videos of dad in his younger days, Jacques is like a carbon copy of dad. This is why she keeps asking for him. The house is so massive with only the two of us." Angel explained.

"Well, what do you insinuate?"

"I was just thinking, and it's merely a suggestion, that Jacques and Catherine can move over to Paris. Catherine can spread her wings and open up another boutique here, and we can do the perfume together. Jacques can open up a new practice here, and can still carry on with locum tenens in London. Catherine's boutique is sorted there. What do you think, Arthur? Look, at her. She doesn't even know that you're here sometimes." she further exclaimed.

"This is just a thought, an idea. Because I am with mom every day. Sometimes I don't want to go out on my own to do my things in the malls, as I don't want to leave her alone. Then I have to wait for Juliette to come. She won't go with me either. Or you can ask Jacques if he would like to join you and Pierre at the company. All I'm saying is, mom, needs him here." Angel said.

"We'll have to speak to him about that. Catherine also has to agree. Those are major, life changes, but not a bad proposal at all. I didn't think of it that way. You are brilliant, sister! I have to get back to the office now. And what if you ask mom if she'd like to visit Jacques and

Catherine in London. Just for now. We will have that talk to Jacques about moving here, another time." Arthur said.

"I will have to ask her. See you later, be good," she said.

Angel asked her mother to go with her to London to Jacques and Catherine. Her face lit up. She was happy and keen to go. Angel was all excited. This will do mom well. Why didn't she think of it, sooner? She booked two open tickets and informed Jacques to pick them up at the airport. They going to be only a few days, but just in case, mom loves it there, they'll stay a little longer. She informed Arthur about the parfum order he can drop off at the house before they leave for London. She will take it along.

Everything was back to normal. Jacques was full-time back at his practice. Catherine's business boomed. Their love for each other grew stronger each day. He had great admiration, strong devotion, and enthusiasm for his love for Catherine. He feels he is ready to commit his life to her. Ready for that plunge.

Jacques stopped by the boutique before he drove to the airport. He had plans for the coming weekend, but very well, then. He can still follow his plan. Mom comes first.

"Hi, I'm going to pick up my mom and Angel at the airport. I was not aware they coming, but I'm glad my mom decides to get out of the house. This will do her good. Is everything okay with you? I suppose Angel staying at your apartment again. I will see you later."

"Oh, that is lovely. I think I can cook your mom a French, dinner. See you later." she laughed.

While driving from the airport, Angel suggested she'll stay at Catherine's place and mom can stay with Jacques. He expected that. But they first stopped at Catherine's.

"Hi, Catherine. You have a beautiful place. I can see why Angel wants to be here. And the lovely cooking? I can smell it a mile away. Jacques really taught you the French cuisine. Magnifique!!"

Gene was already a different person. They could see the difference. Especially, now when she is with Jacques. Maybe, that was all she needed, to get away from home. This is doing great for her, during her trying time and dealing with the loss of her beloved husband. They were married for forty years. She got married before she turned twenty-one. That is a lifetime, together.

"Let's go to the boutique. I want to see, what my daughter has been up to when she's here." Gene said.

On their way to the boutique, Gene remembers the last time she and Francois were in London to visit Jacques, a few years ago. The place looked different. More high risers. The city was very busy, as usual. They entered the boutique.

"Wow, what a fantastic place."

She was introduced to all of Catherine's staff. They were delighted to meet Jacques's, mother. They admired her for her youthfulness and her beauty. Vicky, even jokingly suggested that she could also be a fuller-figure, model, for the in-store. She saw Angel all over the television advertisements. She was modeling Catherine's couture and the parfums.

"Oh, my word, you look gorgeous, like a real, professional supermodel. You have the finesse. I always told you, to take up modeling, but I see this talent was never wasted. Your father would have been so proud of you, my dear. I'm sure he's smiling down on us." mom said.

They went to settle mom in at Jacques's house. The last time she was there, was with her husband. The place still looks the same. The smell in the house, like a strong Oudh diffuser, lingered. Francois loved, Oudh. This brings back their fondest memories to Gene. But when she is with Jacques, she's happy and contented. Then later that evening, they had dinner at Catherine's.

"Jacques, this girl can cook! You in the right hands, my son."

Over, the weekend they had lunch at Catherine's parents' house. Catherine explained to Gene, about the weekly lunch at her parents' house, this was like an occasion to her mother. Gene said to her that the value of family ties influences our lives. Therefore, a family having a solid bond, and an established foundation, with defined values, stand strong. Gene was very happy to meet James and Jemima Darcy. She was telling Jemima, how lonely life has become, without her life partner. She also mentioned, how happy she was to have their daughter in her son's life. They were all delighted to meet Jacques's mother. Jacques thought, he was planning to propose to Catherine over the weekend. His plans were dashed, but in the meantime, he's going to ask her father's permission to marry his daughter. He called Mr. Darcy and Richard to one side of a private space.

"Mr. Darcy, Richard, as you know, I love Catherine with all my heart and soul, and I would love to spend the rest of my life with her. Today, I want to ask you for your permission to marry your daughter. I ask for your blessing? Just before my mom and sister arrived, unexpectedly, I was planning to go away for a weekend to propose to her. As soon as my folks leave, I'm still doing the proposal to her. So, this is in fact, in secrecy that I ask you." Jacques said.

"Oh, my word, Jacques. Catherine isn't just my, daughter, she is my princess. And now a young man asking me to make my princess his queen and you asked for my permission before you even proposed. What a wonderful gesture. You are a good man, Jacques. I knew it since the first time I saw you. I know you will take good care of my baby. I give you, my blessing."

"All the best, Jacques," Richard said smiling.

"Thank you, Sir. Thanks, Richard. It means a lot to me."

They went to join the crowd, having a glorious time with the get-together. Micah also joined them at the lunch. Gene was enjoying her stay in London. They went to the big, massive malls. Gene bought toys for her grandchildren and gifts for Juliette and her sons. They went sightseeing. Every day they did different things.

She also visited a cousin of her husband, who stayed in London. She didn't see her for ages. She was old and fragile. She heard of Francois's passing and was happy to see Gene after a long time. They were close when they were young adults, going out together in their hay days.

Two weeks went by, and they decided to go back to Paris. She was like a brand, new person. There was never a dull moment.

"Thank you, Catherine, for your hospitality, and also thank you for being in my children's life. I love you for this. Jacques taught you the perfect French cooking. Your foods were divine. We shall see you soon." Gene greeted.

They dropped Gene and Angel at the airport.

"We'll see you soon, Catherine." they hugged.

It was early October. Jacques booked a romantic weekend getaway to Saint Tropez, where he was planning to propose to Catherine. Jacques had this passionate state of love, the intense longing for union with her. They both had very powerful feelings for each other. He knew they are soulmates. He was also granted permission from her father, and he has his blessing. So he is on the right page, and he feels so blessed.

He had to do ring shopping and had to choose ring designs. He was thinking, he could have asked Angel to help him decide, while she was there. He opted for the solitaire which appears to be aesthetically appealing as a single dazzling diamond rock. The ring fitted Catherine's description.

The apartment was a penthouse, with a sea view terrace. Jacques has arranged with the hotel staff the setting up of the proposal décor idea for Saturday evening. He asked for a serene and cozy setup with a floral bulb and a decked frame. Table setting with candles and lamps. For dinner, he ordered oysters and seafood platters and champagne on ice. And of course, soft music. He had mixed emotions about this. He feels super excited and nervous at the same time. Not that he'd been in many situations like this before. Catherine was given short notice about the weekend away. He first made sure everything was perfect before he surprised her. She was excited.

They arrived and checked in. This was a beautiful place. They went for a walk down the promenade and did some sightseeing. They went up to the Citadel, which is actually the best spot for sightseeing. They had a light lunch. The food was fantastic. Every dish from salads to desserts. They had three different kinds of pasta, grilled fish, and sauteed prawns. They went on a boat ride. In the afternoon they went scuba diving and snorkeling. When they came back to the penthouse, they were tired of the day's excursion.

He kept the best part for last. Jacques told her they going out for dinner. While she prepared to get ready, Jacques was busy organizing everything to be perfect. Outside on the terrace, the table setting was done, while they were out all day. The foods were delivered in silver domed platters. When she was ready to go, she looked like a million dollars. He couldn't keep his eyes off her.

She thought they were leaving and he just walk her out by the terrace. It was sunset, overlooking the sea.

"Oh, my word Jacques. What a magnificent view. Look at this table. Awe, you're the best. The soft, romantic music was playing. Dinner was already on the table. Without her seeing, he slipped the ring into the glass and poured the Champagne in.

As they drank a toast, she saw the big rock glittering in the glass. He took the sparkling ring out, went on his knee, and popped the question.

"Catherine, I love you with all my heart and every part of my being. I want to spend my entire life with you. Will you marry me?"

By now, Catherine was so thrilled, with her mouth open. She didn't expect this.

"Yes, yes, yes!! You're the love of my life," she shouted excitedly.

"Yes, I will marry you!" she confirmed, a second time.

He slipped the ring on her finger and kissed her. So, they are officially engaged, now. They enjoyed a long romantic night together.

"I can't wait to tell the girls at work. I'm super excited. And Angel, oh my word, she'd be so happy. Can't wait to see her."

"When we leave here, Monday morning, we going straight to my mother, to give her the good news. I can't wait for you to be mine, forever."

"That is so awesome. Thank you for everything, Jacques. I love you with all my heart and soul."

Monday morning, they arrived with a cab at Gene's place. This was a surprise visit. Angel and Gene were happy to see them, unexpectedly.

"Mom, I have asked Catherine, for her hand in marriage," he said shyly.

"Oh, my dear son. That is the best news I've heard in a long time. I'm so happy for you two. You make a perfect match. When I visited you in London, I wanted to ask you when is the big day going to be. What took you so long?" mom laughed.

Angel was over the moon. She called her brothers to drop by and told them of the good news. They had a discussion to do as well.

Pierre and Arthur were just so thrilled, about Jacques and Catherine planning to tie the knot.

Mom Gene was very happy. She made breakfast and Juliette was also there and very excited. When they all arrived, they had a feast. For the first time, since their father passed on, it was pure joy and happiness in the home again. Arthur had to act as the head of the house. He was the eldest, so he had to speak on his father's behalf and be like the father figure.

Angel, couldn't wait for the talk, Arthur promised to have with Jacques.

"Jacques, Arthur needs to talk to you about something, very urgent," Angel said.

"Jacques, we were thinking. The house is so massive here

with only mom and Angel. Would you and Catherine be prepared to move to Paris? This was Angel's suggestion, by the way. Catherine could open a new branch here, with her same clothing designs and the parfum, as well. She has her established business, there. You could also open a new practice here and carry on with the one in London. Going back and forth, you work with locums. This is only a gesture." Arthur mentioned. "Wow, that's a great offer. But we first have to make arrangements, back home." Jacques and Catherine both agreed.

"When are you guys planning to get married? What are you guys waiting for? I'm pretty sure you are both ready. Everything will fall into place. You'll see. No rush, you take your time to decide. I just know that this would make mom very happy." Arthur said.

"Well, regarding moving here, is not an overnight decision to make. But it's a brilliant gesture, and it would be the best for all of us. What do you think, Catherine?" Jacques asked.

"I'm up for any challenge. I will follow what you decide. I think it's a great idea. That sounds appropriate. That can work for me. Everything will stay the same. The only difference is, that we would be based here in Paris. My girls are capable to run the boutique on their own. That place is really special. You could get in permanent locum tenens to continue your practice and start afresh here." she confirmed.

"Unless, Jacques, you can join us at the company, if you like?" Pierre suggested.

"Thank you, brothers. Dentistry is what I specialize in. I don't know anything else. This is my forte. But thanks for the offer, guys. You two carry on. You doing a great job."

"Yay!!! Great vibes are coming. So that is sorted. Let's plan your wedding. I'll be the wedding planner." Angel said excitedly.

"We want to keep it small. Let's set the date for the fourth of November. What do you think Catherine?"

"You set a date with the wedding planner. I'm good with whatever you decide. That's what I also thought. We invite only a few family members and close friends." Catherine said.

"Okay, that would be awesome. Catherine can invite her parents, all her siblings and of course her work colleagues. She can invite the whole of London, we don't mind. We do a small reception, right here in the garden. Juliette can organize the food menu. I'll take care of the decorations and the flowers. I want Zoe to be the little flower girl and Jules and Lois on either side of her." Angel said.

"But, wait. We have a perfect match, here. Catherine has two nieces and a nephew. Bella, Abby, and Ethan. They're all the same ages. So that is just so perfect. We do the three sets of kids and the bride and the groom. Sorted." Angel said smiling.

CHAPTER 12

"In the meantime, mom can invite a few of our immediate aunties and uncles. I'll invite Micah. Pierre or Arthur can be your best man. They can invite some of the people from the company if they like." the wedding planner scheduled.

"That is just perfect. A couple of days, just before the wedding, we can bring my parents and the kids, over. My siblings can come the night before the wedding. Angel, you're a star. I love you." Catherine hugged her.

"We will go back tomorrow and organize our moving home and businesses. She can let all the girls in on our plans and make all the necessary arrangements." Jacques said.

"I also need to make prior arrangements for my patients and inform them. They will definitely miss me, but I will always be around." Jacques said.

There was a sudden sadness showing on Angel's face.

"If only dad could be here with us, to see this magical moment unfold," she said.

"My child, dad is forever watching over us. His spirit is here all the time. I can feel it." mom assured.

"Yes, I know mom." she smiled.

"Ooh la, la, we going to be sisters. I'm so thrilled." Angel was overjoyed.

Gene called Catherine to her room before they left.

"My dear, I would like for you to take Franc's wedding band, for Jacques. Arthur will be the best man, so you can see that he gets it from you."

"Thank you so much. He will love this. I really appreciate it, aunty Gene."

Juliette and Angel started to plan the wedding. They got in the culinary specialist, who offered them to do interactive stations. The big trend is grazing tables. Filling the tables with a variety of different foods also allows the guests to nibble as the day goes on. Light and fresh foods, Sushi Bar, Caprice Skewers, oyster buckets, and the works. She created a beautiful wedding mirror sign written in incursive style,

Welcome to the Wedding of
Jacques and Catherine
2018 November 4

When Catherine was in London, she visited the Evans.

"Hi, mom and dad. I am very happy to have taken your advice. I would like to invite you to be my guests at my wedding in November. Would it be possible? I'd like to have you there. I will pay for the traveling costs and hotel stay. Please say yes."

"Oh wow, that would be awesome!" Mr. Evans said.

"Sure, it would be our honor. We would like to come. Thank you for inviting us."

"Aww thank you, thank you. I'll inform you of the details." Catherine said.

It was the fourth day of November, the wedding day. Catherine's mom and dad with the kids were there two days before. They settled in and the kids enjoyed their holiday stay. All Catherine's family flew in the day before. Her work staff was also there for a couple of days. Micah took off from work for a week, to help Angel with final arrangements.

Angel wanted to have a floral arch with English eucalyptus and large magnolias and cherry blossom branches. They used a mixture of peonies, spray roses, a mixture of hydrangeas, and Avalanche roses. The tables had rose gold table runners, with shimmer sparkled sequin.

Catherine wore a beautiful off-white, Precious long sleeve, Beading sheath, maxi wedding dress with diamante brocade. The train of the dress dragged behind. She had her diamond necklace and earrings on, Jacques bought her. With her Swarovski crystal-embellished designed tiara on her hair made in locks. She looked like a real princess. Jacques wore an elegant black suit, with a silky white shirt and a red tie, his father gave him. They both looked breathtakingly beautiful. Like a fairy tale couple. Everyone met up in the same Saint Germain-des-Pres Cathedral, where the father's memorial service was. They had the same minister who did the memorial. Minister Raphael Fleur Richelieu, who was their father's longtime friend, was doing the marriage vows.

"Do you Jacques take this woman to be your lawfully wedded wife, to live together in matrimony, to love her, comfort her, honor and keep her, in sickness and in health, in sorrow and

joy, to have and to hold, from this day forward, as long as you both shall live."

"I do!" Jacques answered happily with a broad smile.

His big brother Arthur, was his best man and also the ring keeper.

Catherine chose to read her own solemn vow.

"In the name of God, I Catherine Darcy, take you, Jacques Dupont, to be my husband, to have and to hold from this day forward, for better, for worse, for richer, for poorer, in sickness and in health, to love and to cherish, until parted by death. I will love you always and forever."

They did the ring exchanges after the nuptials.

There was a sad moment when they missed their father. Especially moments like this.

"I now pronounce you husband and wife. You may kiss the bride." Minister Rafael said.

It was a beautiful ceremony. The minister mentioned to Jacques that his father said to him a few months ago, that there would be a wedding soon.

"Your father was a good man. His spirit is also here with us today."

"Yes, he was a man in a million. We miss him dearly."

The guests were all invited to the reception at their house in the garden. The three flower girls and petal boys looked like little miniature, brides and grooms. It was a stunning occasion. Such a chic and unique design for the reception.

Everyone congratulated Mr. and Mrs. Jacques Dupont. They wished them long life, with lots of love and happiness, forever after. She was the happiest girl ever. Gene had moved down the hallway, into the guest room. Angel and Juliette had set up the bridal apartment upstairs, very elegantly. Their apartment was decorated with, simple but elaborate décor, everything in white and silver. They had the wedded bliss. Catherine's parents were overwhelmed to see their daughter glowing with happiness. That was all they wanted for her.

"We are so happy for you Mrs. Catherine Darcy Dupont!!" her parents hugged her.

"Congratulations, Catherine. We wish you and your husband the most beautiful life full of love, joy, and happiness, you deserve." Mr. and Mrs. Evans hugged her tightly.

She wanted to cry but put on a brave smile.

"Thank you for being here for me. I appreciate it."

The girls congratulated Catherine. They knew she could do it. They only wanted to see her happy.

Everyone enjoyed the reception.

After the last guests left, they all lend a helping hand in clearing up the wedding reception area. They were all tired of the busy day.

Arthur and Juliette booked the bridal couple a surprise honeymoon to the Bahamas, for one week. The next day, they booked into the Riu Palace Paradise Island. All the honeymoon couples were welcomed with a surprise gift in their rooms. Arthur booked them into a faraway place, so they could be away from work and the hustle and bustle of city life. He wanted them to just relax and take in the serenity of the oceans and be alone, with only their love to share. Pure wedded bliss.

Micah and Rebecca seemed to like each other's company. Catherine's family stayed another day and left afterward. Vicky and the whole entourage left the same night after the wedding.

Catherine arranged for Rebecca to move into her apartment. She and Micah started seeing each other. Micah and Angel remained best friends. Vicky and the other staff continued to manage the boutique in London. She flew back and forth when needed to. Angel went to London to deliver some more perfume orders. Guerlain, Eau de parfum, was the most popular.

After the newlyweds came back from their honeymoon holiday, they first settled in their new home ground. They both loved the change. While the honeymooners were away, Angel was busy scouting around for the best place to open a boutique. There were many options to choose from. Catherine decided on the best place, the Golden Triangle. In the first week of December, they opened a brand, new premises in the busiest part of Paris. Angel was the manageress and they had the same setup, as in London. They employed three ladies to run the boutique. Jacques had contractual locum tenens to be at his London practice. In Paris, he opened a new surgery, in the Saint-Germain-Des-Paris area, close to home. It took him a while to get used to the new working environment. He missed his practice in London and all his patients. He had to fly up and down, quite often.

He did not care, really. As long as he was with the love of his life, nothing else mattered. He was happy that his mom was happy and that was all that was important to him.

Angel was also more involved in her brothers' empire and the perfume business, apart from her own work as a lawyer. Gene was happy and no longer felt alone. She joined clubs and did charity work for churches and underprivileged schools and institutions. She kept busy and enjoyed what she was doing. Gene also worked at the boutique from time to time, when Angel was busy with her own work and Catherine had to go to London.

In February the following year, Catherine was ecstatic, when she announced her pregnancy. She shared her excitement about becoming a mother to all in her family. First, she sent her mom and dad a picture of the ultrasound scan and a message...There's a baby on the way! You are promoted to Grandma and Grandpa!

Gene and all the others were surprised at the dinner table. When she called the girls at work, they were all so happy for her. They advised her to take it easy. Angel would be aunty, again.

Jacques was over the moon. He could not believe he would be a father soon.

Pierre moved on with his life. His boys spend a lot of time with Gene, too. The boys often slept over, in the big house with Gene. Pierre never saw much of Savannah, only when he took his boys to her. Pierre was very awkward whenever he saw Yvonne at family functions. He felt uneasy about Savannah's dirty tricks. Her marriage could have been at stake. But she understood that Pierre was in no way involved in Savannah's underhanded scheming.

Angel bought a variety of baby goods, months before.

Three weeks before Catherine was due, she stayed home. It was, a few nights after all the preparations were done, that Catherine experienced contractions. The pains lasted a few minutes apart from the next contraction. Then her water broke.

Jacques rushed her to the hospital. He was very nervous. He stayed by her side. He was worried sick.

She was in labor for five hours and was only six centimeters dilated. The baby was distressed, so it had to be delivered.

The gynecologist had to perform an emergency cesarean section operation to deliver the baby.

In the early hours of the fourth of November, a beautiful bouncy baby boy was born.

"It's a boy!" Jacques was overwhelmed and emotional when he saw this beautiful creation.

Catherine was still drowsy from the epidural and the strong anesthetics. She opened her eyes slightly to kiss her baby, and it was love at first sight. She was very tired.

"Happy anniversary, Jacques. I love you," she whispered, with lots of pain.

"Oh my, what a beautiful gift. Thank you, Catherine."

She had to stay in hospital for a few days. Everyone came to visit her to see the baby. At home, the Christening ceremony was prepared. Catherine's family flew in to celebrate the birth of the new addition. Everyone was overjoyed. They baptized him, Francois Dupont.

Catherine and Jacques looked at each other with intense emotion. Knowing that seeing their wonderful bundle of joy in front of them, made all the ups and downs, they experienced, worth it.

They were amazed at how much true love can conquer anything. Without saying a word to each other, they fell more in love. They were a family. And baby makes three.

Jacques and Catherine knew they had to create a new perfume, after the birth of their baby. They would name it *L'Armour Vainc Tout.*

EPILOGUE

The love they shared was strong as they moved mountains to be together. They lived happily ever after with the French man's mother, who was extraordinary happy. The divorced brother moved on with his life. The eldest was the father figure to the family. Business was booming. The sister continued with her practice and managing the company. The father's empire continued to grow from strength to strength. There was a new addition to the family. Everything worked out for the best. A brand, new fragrance was on the cards.

ABOUT THE AUTHOR

Kariema Taliep Davids was born and raised in South Africa's wonderful Mother City- Cape Town. She only started writing recently and has self-published two children's picture story books in 2021. She plans to write full time, fulfilling her old passion for writing.

'I love romance. I've been married for 36 years, and I love to also share my personal life experiences and that is relatable to the sub-genre I am planning to write.'

She loves to travel. She lives in Cape Town with her husband, children and grandchildren.

EPILOGUE

The love they shared was strong as they moved mountains to be together. They lived happily ever after with the French man's mother, who was extraordinary happy. The divorced brother moved on with his life. The eldest was the father figure to the family. Business was booming. The sister continued with her practice and managing the company. The father's empire continued to grow from strength to strength. There was a new addition to the family. Everything worked out for the best. A brand, new fragrance was on the cards.

ABOUT
THE AUTHOR

Kariema Taliep Davids was born and raised in South Africa's wonderful Mother City- Cape Town. She only started writing recently and has self-published two children's picture story books in 2021. She plans to write full time, fulfilling her old passion for writing.

'I love romance. I've been married for 36 years, and I love to also share my personal life experiences and that is relatable to the sub-genre I am planning to write.'

She loves to travel. She lives in Cape Town with her husband, children and grandchildren.

www.ingramcontent.com/pod-product-compliance
Lightning Source LLC
Chambersburg PA
CBHW021620270326
41931CB00008B/792